GRADE **3**

Common Core Mathematics

Practice at 3 Levels ●●●

Table of Contents

D0927555

Using This Book

What Is the Common Core?

The Common Core State Standards are an initiative by the states to set shared, consistent, and clear expectations of what students are expected to learn, so teachers and parents know what they need to do to help them. The standards are designed to be rigorous and pertinent to the real world. They reflect the knowledge and skills that our young people need for success in college and careers.

What Are the Intended Outcomes of Common Core?

The goal of the Common Core Standards is to facilitate the following competencies.

Students will:
- demonstrate independence;
- build strong content knowledge;
- respond to the varying demands of audience, task, purpose, and discipline;
- comprehend as well as critique;
- value evidence;
- use technology and digital media strategically and capably;
- come to understand other perspectives and cultures.

What Does This Mean for You?

If your state has joined the Common Core State Standards Initiative, then as a teacher you are required to incorporate these standards into your lesson plans. Your students may need targeted practice in order to meet grade-level standards and expectations and thereby be promoted to the next grade. This book is appropriate for on-grade-level students as well as for intervention, ELs, struggling readers, and special needs. To see if your state has joined the initiative, visit the Common Core States Standards Initiative website to view the most recent adoption map: http://www.corestandards.org/in-the-states.

What Does the Common Core Say Specifically About Math?

For math, the Common Core sets the following key expectations.

- Make sense of problems and persevere in solving them.
- Reason abstractly and quantitatively.
- Construct viable arguments and critique the reasoning of others.
- Model with mathematics.
- Use appropriate tools strategically.
- Attend to precision.
- Look for and make use of structure.
- Look for and express regularity in repeated reasoning.

Common Core Mathematics Grade 3 • ©2012 Newmark Learning, LLC

How Does Common Core Mathematics Help My Students?

- **Mini-lesson for each unit** introduces Common Core math skills and concepts.

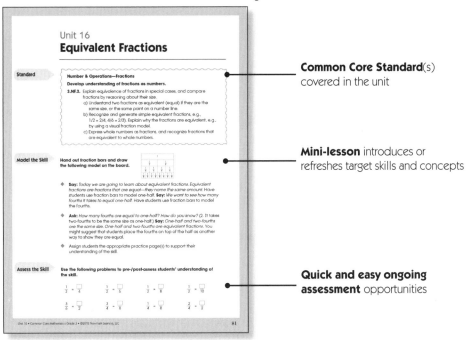

Common Core Standard(s) covered in the unit

Mini-lesson introduces or refreshes target skills and concepts

Quick and easy ongoing assessment opportunities

- **Four practice pages** with three levels of differentiated practice, and word problems follow each mini-lesson.

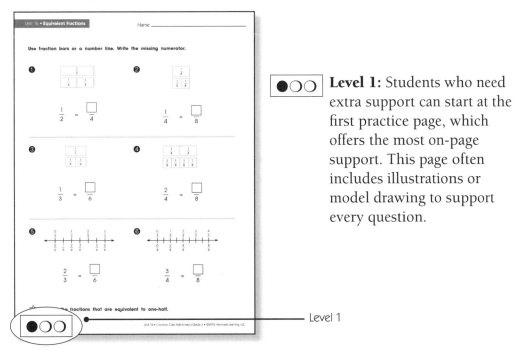

●○○ **Level 1:** Students who need extra support can start at the first practice page, which offers the most on-page support. This page often includes illustrations or model drawing to support every question.

Level 1

●●○ **Level 2:** The second level of practice offers streamlined support features for the first few problems (illustrations, model drawing, or an algorithm reminder for support).

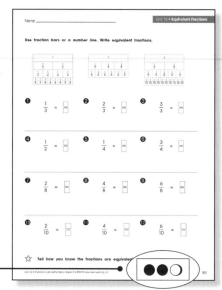

Level 2

☆ Each practice page includes a bonus thinking-skills question so students can answer "How do you know?" to address Common Core Standards of Mathematical Practice and demonstrate their reasoning and understanding of the concept.

●●● **Level 3:** The third practice page does not offer on-page support and depicts how students are expected to be able to perform at this grade level, whether in class or in testing.

☆ **Tell how you find the missing numerator.**

Bonus Thinking Skills question on each practice page

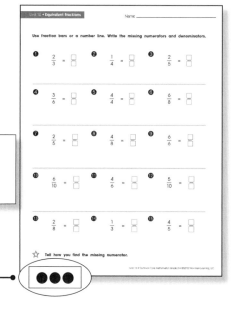

Level 3

Word Problems: Each unit ends with a page of short answer and multiple-choice word problems so students are challenged to marry their computation skills with their quantitative-reasoning and problem-solving skills and grow more familiar with the types of problems they will encounter on standardized tests.

Word Problems

Common Core Standards Alignment Chart • Grade 3

Units	3.NBT.1	3.NBT.2	3.NBT.3	3.OA.1	3.OA.2	3.OA.3	3.OA.4	3.OA.5	3.OA.6-7	3.OA.8	3.OA.9	3.NF.1	3.NF.2	3.NF.3	3.MD.1	3.MD.2	3.MD.3	3.MD.4	3.MD.5	3.MD.6	3.MD.7	3.MD.8	3.G.1	3.G.2
Number & Operations in Base Ten																								
Unit 1: Use Place Value to Round Whole Numbers	✔																							
Unit 2: Estimate Sums and Differences	✔	✔								✔														
Unit 3: Add Whole Numbers		✔																						
Unit 4: Subtract Whole Numbers		✔																						
Operations & Algebraic Thinking																								
Unit 5: Solve Two-Step Word Problems		✔								✔														
Unit 6: Meaning of Multiplication				✔																				
Unit 7: Properties of Multiplication								✔																
Unit 8: Patterns in Multiplication											✔													
Unit 9: Multiply by Multiples of Ten			✔																					
Unit 10: Meaning of Division					✔			✔	✔															
Unit 11: Fact Families for Multiplication & Division									✔															
Unit 12: Solve Multiplication and Division Problems						✔																		
Unit 13: Use Multiplication or Division to Find the Missing Number							✔		✔															
Number & Operations—Fractions																								
Unit 14: Understand Fractions												✔												
Unit 15: Fractions on a Number Line													✔											
Unit 16: Equivalent Fractions														✔										
Unit 17: Compare Fractions														✔										
Measurement & Data and Geometry																								
Unit 18: Time to the Minute															✔									
Unit 19: Grams, Kilograms, Liters																✔								
Unit 20: Measure Length to the Nearest Quarter Inch																		✔						
Unit 21: Make and Use Pictographs																	✔							
Unit 22: Make and Use Bar Graphs																	✔							
Unit 23: Understand Perimeter																						✔		
Unit 24: Understand Area																			✔	✔	✔	✔		
Unit 25: Find Area																			✔	✔	✔	✔		
Unit 26: Quadrilaterals																							✔	
Unit 27: Partition Shapes																								✔

Unit 1
Use Place Value to Round Whole Numbers

Standard

Number & Operations in Base Ten

Use place value understanding and properties of operations to perform multi-digit arithmetic.

3.NBT.1. Use place value understanding to round whole numbers to the nearest 10 or 100.

Model the Skill

Draw the following number line on the board.

- ◆ **Ask:** *How can you use a number line to help you round numbers? Look at the number 42.* (Locate the number on the line and see which ten it is closer to.) Invite students to circle 42 on the number line and determine which ten it is closer to. (40)

- ◆ **Say:** *You can also round numbers to the nearest ten by looking at the ones digits.* **Ask:** *What digit is in the ones place of 42?* (2) *How does that help you round 42?* (If the digit is less than 5, the tens digit stays the same. If it is 5 or greater, the tens digit increases by one.)

- ◆ Assign students the appropriate practice page(s) to support their understanding of the skill.

Assess the Skill

Use the following problems to pre-/post-assess students' understanding of the skill. Have students round each number to the nearest ten and hundred.

75   145   213   382   161   758

Round each number to the nearest ten.

1 63 → _____

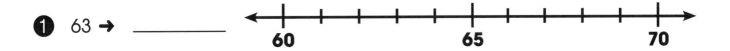

2 45 → _____

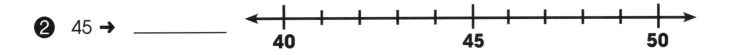

3 106 → _____

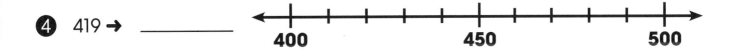

Round each number to the nearest hundred.

4 419 → _____

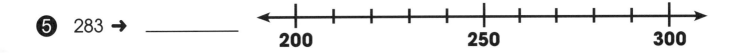

5 283 → _____

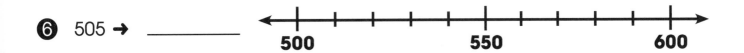

6 505 → _____

 Tell how you round numbers to the nearest ten.

Round each number to the nearest ten.

❶ 623 → _____

❷ 255 → _____

❸ 403 → _____

❹ 527 → _____

Round each number to the nearest hundred.

❺ 843 → _____

❻ 309 → _____

❼ 649 → _____

❽ 950 → _____

☆ **Tell how you round numbers to the nearest hundred.**

Round each number to complete the chart.

	Whole number	Rounded to the nearest ten	Rounded to the nearest hundred
❶	313		
❷	769		
❸	453		
❹	921		
❺	686		
❻	67		
❼	629		
❽	106		
❾	554		
❿		250	200
⓫	938		900
⓬		470	

 Tell how you solved rows 10–12.

Solve.

1 Write three numbers that round to 30 when rounded to the nearest ten.

_____ _____ _____

2 Write three numbers that round to 100 when rounded to the nearest hundred.

_____ _____ _____

3 Write three numbers that round to 70 when rounded to the nearest ten.

_____ _____ _____

4 Write three numbers that round to 400 when rounded to the nearest hundred.

_____ _____ _____

Circle the letter for the correct answer.

5 What number can round to 760 when it rounds to the nearest ten and 800 when it rounds to the nearest hundred?

a) 751

b) 763

c) 754

d) 768

6 What number rounds to 500 when it rounds to the nearest ten and to the nearest hundred?

a) 507

b) 491

c) 540

d) 504

Unit 2
Estimate Sums and Differences

Standard

Number & Operations in Base Ten

Use place value understanding and properties of operations to perform multi-digit arithmetic.

3.NBT.1. Use place value understanding to round whole numbers to the nearest 10 or 100.

3.NBT.2. Fluently add and subtract within 1,000 using strategies and algorithms based on place value, properties of operations, and/or the relationship between addition and subtraction.

Model the Skill

Write the following problem on the board.

$$27 + 42 =$$

◆ **Say:** *Today we are going to estimate sums and differences. A sum is the total when you add. A difference is the amount that is left when you subtract. Look at this problem. Will you round the addends to the nearest ten or nearest hundred? Why?* (Answer: ten because the addends are much less than 100)

◆ **Ask:** *How can you use rounding to estimate the sum of 27 and 42?* (Round 27 to 30 and 42 to 40. Then add 30 and 40 to get 70.) *Why might rounding numbers to the nearest ten make it easier to add?* (Possible answer: It is easy to add tens.)

◆ Assign students the appropriate practice page(s) to support their understanding of the skill.

Assess the Skill

Use the following problems to pre-/post-assess students' understanding of the skill. Have students round each addend to the nearest ten or hundred and then find the sum or difference.

65	85	315	465	841
+ 27	− 17	+ 178	− 189	− 96

Name _____

Round each number to the nearest ten. Then estimate the sum or difference.

❶
$$23 \rightarrow \boxed{}$$
$$+\ 38 \rightarrow +\boxed{}$$

❷
$$72 \rightarrow \boxed{}$$
$$-\ 15 \rightarrow -\boxed{}$$

❸
$$57 \rightarrow \boxed{}$$
$$-\ 29 \rightarrow -\boxed{}$$

❹
$$141 \rightarrow \boxed{}$$
$$-\ 37 \rightarrow -\boxed{}$$

❺
$$68 \rightarrow \boxed{}$$
$$+\ 57 \rightarrow +\boxed{}$$

❻
$$345 \rightarrow \boxed{}$$
$$-\ 86 \rightarrow -\boxed{}$$

Round each number to the nearest hundred. Then estimate the sum or difference.

❼
$$116 \rightarrow \boxed{}$$
$$+\ 82 \rightarrow +\boxed{}$$

❽
$$267 \rightarrow \boxed{}$$
$$-\ 145 \rightarrow -\boxed{}$$

❾
$$381 \rightarrow \boxed{}$$
$$-\ 217 \rightarrow -\boxed{}$$

☆ **Tell how you rounded for Problem 9.**

●○○

Round each number to the nearest ten. Then estimate the sum or difference.

1
302 →
+ 204 → +

2
192 →
− 95 → −

3
681 →
− 217 → −

4
323
− 267

5
286
+ 579

6
764
− 397

7
203
+ 373

8
452
− 236

9
774
+ 189

10
406
+ 328

11
709
− 166

12
227
+ 364

13
423
− 171

14
89
+ 516

15
964
− 108

☆ **Tell how you estimated the sum for Problem 14.**

Name _____

Round each number to the nearest ten. Then estimate the sum or difference.

1   149
      + 318

2   452
      − 39

3   278
      + 337

4   488
      + 325

5   346
      − 175

6   227
      + 579

7   988
      − 269

8   764
      − 397

9   167
      + 153

10   308
       − 149

11   834
       + 109

12   414
       + 299

13   318
       + 423

14   781
       − 119

15   66
       + 385

16   207
       + 484

17   847
       − 175

18   389
       + 232

19   905
       − 368

20   613
       − 87

☆   **Write how you estimated the sum for Problem 18.**

Solve.

1 Eva has 183 beads. She uses 37 beads to make a necklace. About how many beads does she have left over?

_____ beads

2 Rory has 132 baseball cards in his collection. His grandfather gives him 175 more cards. About how many cards does he now have in his collection?

_____ baseball cards

3 Last week's groceries cost 134 dollars. This week's groceries cost 158 dollars. About how much did the groceries cost in all?

_____ dollars

4 Collette has 246 stickers. She gives 28 to her brother. About how many stickers does Collette have left?

_____ stickers

Circle the letter for the correct answer.

5 Which problem has a sum of about 800?

a) 523 – 307

b) 523 + 307

c) 442 + 322

d) 496 + 402

6 Which problem has a difference of about 70?

a) 764 – 632

b) 64 + 134

c) 278 – 205

d) 489 – 411

Unit 3
Add Whole Numbers

Number & Operations in Base Ten

Use place value understanding and properties of operations to perform multi-digit arithmetic.

3.NBT.2. Fluently add and subtract within 1,000 using strategies and algorithms based on place value, properties of operations, and/or the relationship between addition and subtraction.

Model the Skill

Hand out base-ten blocks and write the following problem on the board.

$$\begin{array}{r} 42 \\ + 29 \\ \hline \end{array}$$

◆ **Say:** *We are going to add today. We are going to find the sum. A sum is the total amount. How many ones are there in all?* (11) Allow students to count or add the ones. Record the ones in the vertical addition.

◆ **Ask:** *How many tens are there in all?* (7) Record the tens. **Ask:** *What is the sum of 42 + 29?* (71) Help students connect the models to the standard algorithm by adding the ones first. Accept other ways to find the sum.

◆ **Ask:** *How did you find the answer? How many ones are there in all?* (11) *Did you have to regroup the ones?* (yes) *After you regrouped the ones into ten and one, how many tens are there in all?* (7) *What is the sum?* (71)

◆ Assign students the appropriate practice page(s) to support their understanding of the skill.

Assess the Skill

Use the following problems to pre-/post-assess students' understanding of the skill.

$$\begin{array}{r} 56 \\ + 39 \\ \hline \end{array} \qquad \begin{array}{r} 227 \\ + 168 \\ \hline \end{array} \qquad \begin{array}{r} 605 \\ + 128 \\ \hline \end{array} \qquad \begin{array}{r} 581 \\ + 234 \\ \hline \end{array}$$

Name _____

Find the sum for each problem.

1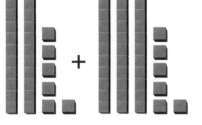

$$\begin{array}{r} 26 \\ + 36 \\ \hline \end{array}$$

26 + 36

2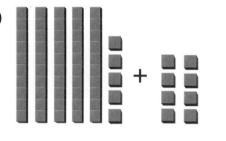

$$\begin{array}{r} 55 \\ + 8 \\ \hline \end{array}$$

55 + 8

3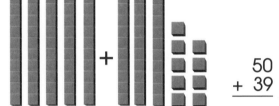

$$\begin{array}{r} 50 \\ + 39 \\ \hline \end{array}$$

50 + 39

4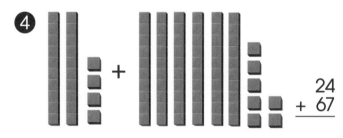

$$\begin{array}{r} 24 \\ + 67 \\ \hline \end{array}$$

24 + 67

5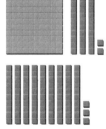

hundreds	tens	ones
1	3	2
+	9	3

132 + 93

6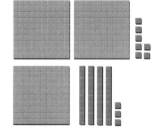

hundreds	tens	ones
2	0	7
+ 1	4	3

207 + 143

 Circle the problem where you regrouped the tens.

Name _____

Find the sum for each problem.

1   346
      + 122

hundreds	tens	ones
3	4	6
+ 1	2	2

2   226
      + 43

3   323
      + 44

4   681
      + 217

5   107
      + 16

6   151
      + 54

7   206
      + 98

8   314
      + 37

9   720
      + 81

10   476
       + 101

11   313 + 256

12   507 + 184

13   375 + 246

14   508 + 132

15   79 + 644

16   264 + 708

 Tell how you know your answer is reasonable.

Name _____

Find the sum for each problem.

1   586
       + 13

2   204
       + 46

3   118
       + 343

4   600
       + 286

5   245 + 132

6   586 + 213

7   421 + 369

8   355 + 273

9   300 + 675

10   266 + 128

11   73 + 643

12   564 + 206

13   546 + 216

14   354 + 165

15   67 + 812

16   301 + 129

17   392 + 135

18   209 + 372

19   272 + 437

20   613 + 208

 Write the steps you follow to add multi-digit numbers.

Name _____

Solve.

1 The lawn mower costs 329 dollars. The hedge clippers cost 178 dollars. How much do the tools cost in all?

2 Reeve scored 453 points the first time she played her new video game. She scored 518 points the second time she played. What is her combined score?

3 Sam has 373 craft sticks. He buys a box of 425 more craft sticks. How many sticks does Sam have in all?

4 Abby walks 146 yards to school from her house. The library is another 456 yards from school. What is the distance in yards from Abby's house to the library?

Circle the letter for the correct answer.

5 Helen needs 152 sequins for her costume. Freddie needs 209 sequins for his costume. How many sequins do they need in all?

a) 361

b) 351

c) 461

d) 261

6 Joanie has 387 pumpkin seeds. Harrison has 562 pumpkin seeds. How many pumpkin seeds do they have in all?

a) 849

b) 949

c) 739

d) 938

Unit 4
Subtract Whole Numbers

Standard

Number & Operations in Base Ten

Use place value understanding and properties of operations to perform multi-digit arithmetic.

3.NBT.2. Fluently add and subtract within 1,000 using strategies and algorithms based on place value, properties of operations, and/or the relationship between addition and subtraction.

Model the Skill

Write the following problems on the board.

$$\begin{array}{r} 57 \\ -\ 26 \\ \hline \end{array} \qquad \begin{array}{r} 65 \\ -\ 17 \\ \hline \end{array}$$

◆ **Say:** *We are going to subtract today. We are going to find the difference. Look at the first problem on the board. How many ones are there in the number 57?* (7) *How many ones are you going to take away?* (6) Allow students to record the difference.

◆ **Ask:** *How many tens are there in 57?* (5) *How many tens are you going to take away?* (2) Allow students to record the remaining tens. (3) **Ask:** *What is the difference of 57 – 26?* (31)

◆ **Say:** *Look at the next problem. What happens when you subtract the ones?* Students should recognize that there are not enough ones to subtract and therefore they must regroup. Discuss how to regroup and record the regrouped ten. **Ask:** *How many ones and tens are left after subtracting?* (8 ones, 4 tens) *What is the difference?* (48)

◆ Assign students the appropriate practice page(s) to support their understanding of the skill.

Assess the Skill

Use the following problems to pre-/post-assess students' understanding of the skill.

$$\begin{array}{r} 48 \\ -\ 29 \\ \hline \end{array} \qquad \begin{array}{r} 185 \\ -\ 118 \\ \hline \end{array} \qquad \begin{array}{r} 307 \\ -\ 126 \\ \hline \end{array} \qquad \begin{array}{r} 465 \\ -\ 346 \\ \hline \end{array}$$

Name _____

Find the difference for each problem.

1

$$\begin{array}{r} 35 \\ -\ 14 \\ \hline \end{array}$$

35 – 14

2

$$\begin{array}{r} 43 \\ -\ 23 \\ \hline \end{array}$$

43 – 23

3

$$\begin{array}{r} 64 \\ -\ 25 \\ \hline \end{array}$$

64 – 25

4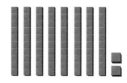

$$\begin{array}{r} 82 \\ -\ 34 \\ \hline \end{array}$$

82 – 34

5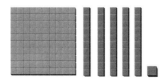

151 – 128

	hundreds	tens	ones
	1	5	1
-	1	2	8

6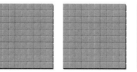

307 – 143

	hundreds	tens	ones
	3	0	7
-	1	4	3

☆ **Circle the problems where you had to regroup the ones.**

Name _____

Find the difference for each problem.

1

$$\begin{array}{r} 238 \\ -\ 23 \\ \hline \end{array}$$

238 − 23

2 475 − 65

hundreds	tens	ones
4	7	5
−	6	5

3
$$\begin{array}{r} 187 \\ -\ 51 \\ \hline \end{array}$$

4
$$\begin{array}{r} 409 \\ -\ 108 \\ \hline \end{array}$$

5
$$\begin{array}{r} 246 \\ -\ 125 \\ \hline \end{array}$$

6
$$\begin{array}{r} 641 \\ -\ 322 \\ \hline \end{array}$$

7
$$\begin{array}{r} 341 \\ -\ 221 \\ \hline \end{array}$$

8
$$\begin{array}{r} 352 \\ -\ 307 \\ \hline \end{array}$$

9
$$\begin{array}{r} 427 \\ -\ 64 \\ \hline \end{array}$$

10
$$\begin{array}{r} 754 \\ -\ 383 \\ \hline \end{array}$$

11
$$\begin{array}{r} 608 \\ -\ 218 \\ \hline \end{array}$$

12 321 − 30

13 800 − 136

14 784 − 365

 Tell how you know your answer is reasonable.

Name _____

Find the difference for each problem.

1 246
     − 122

2 208
     − 46

3 718
     − 343

4 800
     − 278

5 354 − 165

6 680 − 645

7 409 − 73

8 549 − 256

9 421 − 369

10 392 − 128

11 783 − 674

12 586 − 213

13 437 − 206

14 354 − 272

15 861 − 812

16 992 − 875

17 400 − 204

18 909 − 372

19 772 − 437

20 613 − 318

☆ **Write the steps you took to solve Problem 18.**

Find the difference for each problem.

1 The lawn mower costs 329 dollars. The hedge clippers cost 178 dollars. How much more does the lawn mower cost?

2 Reeve scored 453 points the first time she played her new video game. She scored 618 points the second time she played. By how many points did her score improve the second time?

3 Sam has 875 craft sticks. He uses 798 sticks to build a model. How many sticks does Sam have left?

4 Abby walks 146 yards to school from her house. The park is 655 yards from her house. How much farther is the park from her house compared to the school?

Circle the letter for the correct answer.

5 Helen needs 152 sequins for her costume. Freddie needs 209 sequins for his costume. How many more sequins does Freddie need?

a) 47

b) 57

c) 67

d) 157

6 Joanie has 387 pumpkin seeds. Harrison has 562 pumpkin seeds. How many more pumpkin seeds does Harrison have?

a) 225

b) 185

c) 285

d) 175

Unit 5
Solve Two-Step Word Problems

Standard

Operations & Algebraic Thinking

Solve problems involving the four operations, and identify and explain patterns in arithmetic.

3.OA.8. Solve two-step word problems using the four operations. Represent these problems using equations with a letter standing for the unknown quantity. Assess the reasonableness of answers using mental computation and estimation strategies including rounding.

Model the Skill

Hand out counters and write the following problem on the board.

Sam has 3 apples and some bananas.
He has 8 pieces of fruit in all.
How many bananas does Sam have?

$$3 + b = 8$$

◆ **Say:** *Today we are going to solve problems that use a letter to stand for an unknown quantity. Look at this word problem. What do we know?* (Sam has 3 apples and some bananas. He has 8 pieces of fruit in all.) *What do we need to find out?* (how many bananas Sam has) *What letter should we use to represent the number of bananas?* (b) Point out that any letter can be used to represent an unknown quantity.

◆ Using red counters, model the apples. Ask a volunteer to add yellow counters to make a total of 8. **Ask:** *How many apples are there?* (3) *How many bananas did we add to make 8 pieces of fruit in all?* (5) *How many counters are there in all?* (8)

◆ Assign students the appropriate practice page(s) to support their understanding of the skill.

Assess the Skill

Use the following problems to pre-/post-assess students' understanding of the skill.

Lila has 6 strawberries. She eats 1. Then she gives 3 away. How many strawberries does she have left?

The orchard had 8 rows of apple trees. There were 7 trees in each row. 2 trees were cut down after they were damaged in a storm. How many trees are remaining in the orchard?

Write the missing numbers.

1 Tomas has a dozen eggs. He uses some eggs to make breakfast. After breakfast, he has 9 eggs left. How many eggs did he use?

$12 - e = 9$

$12 -$ _____ $= 9$

$e =$ _____

Tomas used _____ eggs.

2 Philip baked 36 cookies. Caden ate 2 cookies. Riley ate 4 cookies. How many cookies does Philip have left?

$36 - 2 = 34$

$34 - 4 = c$

$c =$ _____

Philip has _____ cookies left.

3 Ana read 9 pages of a book. Robert read twice as many pages. How many pages did they read in all?

$2 \times 9 =$ _____

$9 + 18 =$ _____

$p =$ _____

They read _____ pages in all.

4 Sara picks 17 string beans. Paula picks 16 string beans. They each give 4 string beans to Tim. What is the total number of string beans that Sara and Paula have left?

$(17 - 4) + (16 - 4) = b$

$13 \ + \ 12 =$ _____

$b =$ _____

Sara and Paula have _____ string beans.

☆ **Circle the problem where you used multiplication.**

Name _____

Write the missing numbers.

1 Lily bakes 8 muffins. She bakes 4 more. She gives 3 muffins to her friends. How many muffins (*m*) does she have now?

$8 + 4 - 3 = m$

$8 + 4 - 3 =$ _____

$m =$ _____

Lily has _____ muffins now.

2 Renee invites 14 guests to her party. Her mom invites 2 more guests. 5 people cannot come. How many guests (*g*) will be at the party?

$14 + 2 - 5 = g$

$14 + 2 - 5 =$ _____

$g =$ _____

There will be _____ guests at the party.

3 Ms. Green picked vegetables from her garden. She picked some tomatoes, 7 carrots, and 5 peppers. She picked 19 vegetables in all. How many tomatoes (*t*) did she pick?

Ms. Green picked ____ tomatoes.

4 Sophie had 17 apples. Mark had 15 apples. They used 8 apples to bake a pie. How many apples (*a*) do they have left?

They have ____ apples left.

5 Addie has 8 plates. Jose has twice as many plates as Addie.

How many plates does Jose have? _____

How many more plates does Jose have compared with Addie? _____

How many plates do they have in all? _____

 Tell how you solved Problem 2.

●●○

Name _____

Solve.

1 Lucy had 18 apples. She gave 6 to Eric and some to Sue. She has 5 apples left. How many apples did she give to Sue?

$n =$ _____

2 Sasha's baseball team played 16 games. The team won 9 games and tied 2 games. How many games did the team lose?

$n =$ _____

3 Callie read 8 pages of a book on Monday. She read 9 pages on Tuesday. She read the rest of the book on Wednesday. There are 32 pages in the book. How many pages did she read on Wednesday?

$n =$ _____

4 Fred has some blue pens. He has 9 black pens and 5 red pens. He has 25 pens in all. How many blue pens does he have?

$n =$ _____

5 Joseph has 6 stickers. Rachel has three times as many stickers as Joseph.

How many stickers does Rachel have? _____

How many more stickers does Rachel have than Joseph?

_____

How many stickers do they have in all? _____

6 Finbar has 67 craft sticks. Lindsay has 45 sticks. They will use 52 sticks to build a model.

How many more sticks does Finbar have? _____

What is the total number of craft sticks they have? _____

How many sticks will they have left after they build their model? _____

 Explain how you solved Problem 4.

Name _____

**Write a number sentence to solve the problem.
Then solve the problem.**

1 There are 3 apples, 4 pears, and 6 bananas in a fruit bowl. How many pieces of fruit are in the bowl?

2 Kit has some green balloons, 6 yellow balloons, and 5 blue balloons. She has 20 balloons in all. How many green balloons (n) does she have?

3 Marie runs 11 miles in three days. She runs 3 miles on each of the first two days. How many miles does she run on the third day?

4 Evan baked 8 bran muffins and 7 blueberry muffins. He gave 3 of his muffins to a friend. How many muffins (n) does Evan have left?

Circle the letter for the correct answer.

5 There are 3 apple tarts and twice as many peach tarts. How many tarts are there in all?

a) 9

b) 8

c) 6

d) 5

6 Carla has 4 rows of rose bushes in her garden. Each row has 6 bushes. If she plants one more row of 6 bushes, how many rose bushes will she have?

a) 10

b) 16

c) 24

d) 30

Unit 6
Meaning of Multiplication

Standard

Operations & Algebraic Thinking

Represent and solve problems involving multiplication and division.

3.OA.1. Interpret products of whole numbers, e.g., interpret 5 X 7 as the total number of objects in 5 groups of 7 objects each. For example, describe a context in which a total number of objects can be expressed as 5 X 7.

Model the Skill

Hand out counters.

◆ **Say:** *We are going to see how addition and multiplication are related.* Have students use counters to model 4 groups of 3.

◆ **Ask:** *How many equal groups do you have?* (4) *How many counters are there in each group?* (3) *How many counters are there in all?* (12)

◆ **Say:** *You can record 4 groups of 3 as an addition sentence or as a multiplication sentence.* Have students record the sum and the product. **Ask:** *What is the sum of 3 + 3 + 3 + 3?* (12) *What is the product of 4 x 3?* (12) *Remember, to multiply you need equal groups.*

◆ Assign students the appropriate practice page(s) to support their understanding of the skill.

Assess the Skill

Use the following problems to pre-/post-assess students' understanding of the skill.

$4 + 4 + 4 =$ _____

$3 \times 4 =$ _____

$6 + 6 =$ _____

$2 \times 6 =$ _____

Name _____

Write the missing numbers.

1   4 + 4 + 4 = _____

_____ groups of _____

3 x 4 = _____

2   4 + 4 + 4 + 4 + 4 = _____

_____ groups of _____

5 x 4 = _____

3   6 + 6 = _____

_____ groups of _____

2 x 6 = _____

4   5 + 5 + 5 + 5 = _____

_____ groups of _____

4 x 5 = _____

5   7 + 7 + 7 = _____

_____ groups of _____

3 x 7 = _____

6   6 + 6 + 6 + 6 = _____

_____ groups of _____

4 x 6 = _____

☆   **Tell how the addition sentence and the multiplication sentence are the same.**

Name _____

**Use counters to model the problem. Draw a picture to show your work.
Complete each number sentence.**

1 4 groups of 3

3 + 3 + 3 + 3 = _____

4 x 3 = _____

2 2 groups of 8

8 + 8 = _____

2 x 8 = _____

3 3 groups of 5

5 + 5 + 5 = _____

3 x 5 = _____

4 4 groups of 5

5 + 5 + 5 + 5 = _____

4 x 5 = _____

5 6 groups of 2

2 + 2 + 2 + 2 + 2 + 2 = _____

6 x 2 = _____

6 3 groups of 6

6 + 6 + 6 = _____

3 x 6 = _____

 Tell how the number sentences both describe your picture.

Name _____

Draw a picture for each multiplication sentence. Describe the picture. Then find the product.

1   5 x 2 = _____

2   4 x 5 = _____

_____

_____

3   6 x 4 = _____

4   8 x 2 = _____

_____

_____

5   3 x 7 = _____

6   4 x 9 = _____

_____

_____

   Write about the steps you took to find the product.

Solve.

1 There are 3 equal groups of apples. Each group has 5 apples. How many apples are there in all?

2 There are 4 bowls of plums. Each bowl has 3 plums. How many plums are there in all?

3 Erin runs 6 miles each day for 3 days. How many miles does she run in all? Write an addition sentence and a multiplication sentence that shows the total.

4 There are 4 pans of muffins. Each pan has 6 muffins. How many muffins are there in all?

Circle the letter for the correct answer.

5 There are 5 trays of pies. Each tray has 4 pies. Which expression can be used to show the total number of pies?

a) 4 + 5
b) 4 + 4 + 4 + 4
c) 5 x 4
d) 5 x 5 x 5 x 5

6 There are 7 people fishing at the lake. Each person catches 3 fish. What is the total number of fish caught?

a) 10
b) 14
c) 20
d) 21

Unit 7
Properties of Multiplication

Standard

Operations & Algebraic Thinking

Understand properties of multiplication and the relationship between multiplication and division.

3.OA.5. Apply properties of operations as strategies to multiply and divide (i.e.: commutative property of multiplication, associative property of multiplication, and distributive property).

Model the Skill

Hand out counters.

◆ Have students use counters to model the commutative property of multiplication. **Say:** *Today we are going to multiply two numbers and then change the order of the numbers to see if the product will change.* Have students model along as you demonstrate how to show 3 x 2 with counters.

◆ **Ask:** *How many groups of counters are there? How many counters are in each group? What is the product of 3 x 2?*

◆ **Say:** *Now let's see what happens to the product when we change the order of the numbers.* Guide students to model 2 x 3. **Ask:** *How many groups of counters are there? How many counters are there in each group? What is the product of 2 x 3? Does changing the order of the numbers change the product? (no) If you know 3 x 2 = 6, then you know 2 x 3 = 6.*

◆ Assign students the appropriate practice page(s) to support their understanding of the skill.

Assess the Skill

Use the following problems to pre-/post-assess students' understanding of the skill.

3 x 4 = _____   2 x (2 x 3) = _____

4 x 6 = _____   (2 x 2) x 3 = _____

5 x 7 = _____   4 x (2 x 2) = _____

8 x 8 = _____   (4 x 2) x 2 = _____

Solve.

1

△△△△△
△△△△△
△△△△△
△△△△△
△△△△

5 x 4 = _____

△△△△△
△△△△△
△△△△△
△△△△△

4 x 5 = _____

2

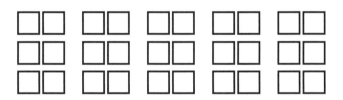

(3 x 2) x 5
6 x 5 = _____

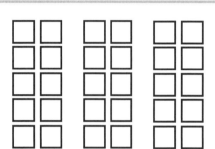

3 x (2 x 5)
3 x 10 = _____

Draw a line to separate the counters to match the numbers.
Write the product.

3 2 x 9
(2 x 5) + (2 x 4)
2 x 9 = _____

4 4 x 8
(4 x 4) + (4 x 4)
4 x 8 = _____

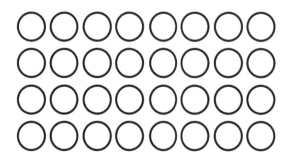

☆ **Pick two numbers. Tell about the product when the order is changed.**

 37

Name _____

Use counters to model each problem. Write a number sentence for each problem.

❶

4 x 2 = _____   2 x 4 = _____

❷

△△△△△△
△△△△△△
△△△△△△
△△△△△△

△△△△ △△△△
△△△△ △△△△
△△△△ △△△△

4 x 6 = _____   6 x 4 = _____

❸ (2 x 2) x 4   2 x (2 x 4)

_____ x 4 = _____   2 x _____ = _____

❹ (2 x 5) x 2   2 x (5 x 2)

   10   x 2 = _____   2 x   10   = _____

❺ 5 x 7   **❻** 6 x 9

(5 x 3) + (5 x 4)   (6 x 5) + (6 x 4)

_____ + _____ = _____   _____ + _____ = _____

5 x 7 = _____   6 x 9 = _____

❼ 4 x 8   **❽** 3 x 7

(4 x 4) + (4 x 4)   (3 x 3) + (3 x 4)

_____ + _____ = _____   _____ + _____ = _____

4 x 8 = _____   3 x 7 = _____

☆ **Pick three numbers. Tell about the product when the grouping is changed.**

Name _____

Write two true multiplication sentences for each model.

❶

_____

_____

❷

_____

_____

Show two ways to solve each problem.

❸ 2 x 2 x 3

_____ X _____ = _____

_____ X _____ = _____

❹ 2 x 4 x 3

_____ X _____ = _____

_____ X _____ = _____

❺ 4 x 2 x 3

_____ X _____ = _____

_____ X _____ = _____

❻ 2 x 3 x 3

_____ X _____ = _____

_____ X _____ = _____

Fill in the missing number to find the product.

❼ 5 x 9

(5 x 5) + (5 x _____)

_____ + _____ = _____

5 x 9 = _____

❽ 2 x 9

(2 x _____) + (2 x 4)

_____ + _____ = _____

2 x 9 = _____

❾ 7 x 8

(7 x _____) + (7 x _____)

_____ + _____ = _____

7 x 8 = _____

❿ 8 x 9

(8 x _____) + (8 x _____)

_____ + _____ = _____

8 x 9 = _____

☆ **Write about how you solved Problem 10.**

Solve.

1 There are 8 rows of apple trees. Each row has 7 trees. Write two multiplication sentences that show the total number of apple trees.

2 There are 8 pots of corn. Each pot has 6 corn cobs. Write two multiplication sentences to show the total number of corn cobs.

3 There are 5 bags of beets. Each bag has 4 beets. Write two multiplication sentences to show the total number of beets.

4 There are 2 bakers. Each baker has 4 pans. Each pan has 6 cupcakes. Write 2 expressions that show the total number of cupcakes.

Circle the letter for the correct answer.

5 Which expression is equal to 4 x 8 ?

a) (4 x 5) + (4 x 3)

b) 8 x 4

c) (4 x 4) + (4 x 4)

d) all of the above

6 There are 2 buses. There are 7 girls and 3 boys on each bus. Which expression shows the total number of boys and girls on the buses?

a) 3 x (7 + 2)

b) 2 x (7 + 3)

c) (2 + 3) x 7

d) 2 + 3 + 7

     Unit 7 • Common Core Mathematics Grade 3 • ©2012 Newmark Learning, LLC

Unit 8
Patterns in Multiplication

Standard

Operations & Algebraic Thinking

Explain patterns in arithmetic.

3.OA.9. Identify arithmetic patterns, and explain them using properties of operations. For example, observe that 4 times a number is always even, and explain why 4 times a number can be decomposed into two equal addends.

Model the Skill

Hand out counters and write the following problem on the board.

$$1 \times 3 = 3$$

◆ Have students use counters to model the problem. **Say:** *Today we are going to look for patterns when we multiply.* Have students model along as you demonstrate how to show 1 x 3 with counters.

◆ **Ask:** *How many groups of counters are there? How many counters are there in the group? What is the product of 1 x 3?*

◆ **Say:** *Now let's try multiplying other numbers by 1. What pattern do you see when we multiply with 1?* (Possible response: The product is always the other factor.)

◆ Follow a similar process for multiplying by zero. **Ask:** *Why don't you need counters to model 0 x 3?* (Possible response: because there are 0 groups of 3, which means you don't need any counters)

◆ Assign students the appropriate practice page(s) to support their understanding of the skill.

Assess the Skill

Use the following problems to pre-/post-assess students' understanding of the skill.

Write the following patterns on the board and ask students to complete each pattern and then define the rule for each pattern.

2, 4, 6, ___, ___, 12, ___, 16 ___, 20

3, 6, ___, ___, 15, ___, 21 ___, 27, ___, 33, ___

16, 20, ___, 28, ___, ___, 40, 44

12, 18, ___, 30, ___, 42, ___, ___

Name _____

Write each product.

1 1 x 0 = _____

    1 x 1 = _____ □

    1 x 2 = _____ ☆☆

    1 x 3 = _____ ○○○

    1 x 4 = _____ □□□□

    1 x 5 = _____ ☆☆☆☆☆

    1 x 6 = _____ ○○○○○○

    1 x 7 = _____ □□□□□□□

    1 x 8 = _____ ☆☆☆☆☆☆☆☆

2 0 x 1 = _____

    0 x 2 = _____

    0 x 3 = _____

    0 x 4 = _____

    0 x 5 = _____

    0 x 6 = _____

    0 x 7 = _____

    0 x 8 = _____

    0 x 9 = _____

---

3 2 x 1 = _____ □□
                   ☆☆

    2 x 2 = _____ ☆☆

    2 x 3 = _____ ○○○
                   ○○○

    2 x 4 = _____ □□□□
                   □□□□

    2 x 5 = _____ ☆☆☆☆☆
                   ☆☆☆☆☆

    2 x 6 = _____ ○○○○○○
                   ○○○○○○

    2 x 7 = _____ □□□□□□□
                   □□□□□□□

    2 x 8 = _____ ☆☆☆☆☆☆☆☆
                   ☆☆☆☆☆☆☆☆

4 3 x 1 = _____

    3 x 2 = _____

    3 x 3 = _____

    3 x 4 = _____

    3 x 5 = _____

    3 x 6 = _____

    3 x 7 = _____

    3 x 8 = _____

☆ **Circle the pattern where the product is always zero.**

Name _____

Look for patterns. Then complete each table.

1

Number of Bicycles	1	2	3	4	5	6
Number of Wheels	2	4	6			

2

Number of Nickels	1	2	3	4	5	6
Number of Cents	5	10	15			

3

Number of Chairs	1	2	3	4	5	6
Number of Legs	4	8				

4

Number of Insects	1	2	3		5	6
Number of Legs	6		18			

5

Number of Gallons	1	2	3	4	5	6
Number of Pints	8	16			40	

6

Number of Centimeters	1	2	3	4	5	6
Number of Millimeters	10	20	30			

7

Number of Tricycles	0	1	2	3	4	5
Number of Wheels	0	3				

8

Number of Skateboards	0	2	4	6	8	10
Number of Wheels	0	8				

 Tell about the patterns in the Table 8.

Name _____

Complete the multiplication table.

x	0	1	2	3	4	5	6	7	8	9	10
0	0		0		0		0	0		0	0
1		1	2	3		5		7			
2	0	2	4		8						20
3		3		9							
4	0		8					28			
5		5								45	
6	0						36				
7		7		21				49			
8	0								64		
9							54				
10	0			30							100

☆ Write about the patterns you see in the table.

Solve.

1 What is the product when one of the factors in a multiplication sentence is zero?

2 Which row in the multiplication table has the numbers 6, 12, 18, and 21?

3 Describe the pattern in the table below.

Number of Centimeters	1	2	3	4	5	6
Number of Millimeters	10	20	30			

Circle the letter for the correct answer.

4 There are 6 bookshelves. Each bookshelf has 8 books. Which expression can be used to show the total number of books?

a) 8 + 6

b) 8 + 8 + 8 + 8 + 8 + 8

c) 8 x 6

d) 6 x 6 x 6 x 6

5 There are 4 wheels on each stroller. The store has 20 strollers. How many wheels are in the stroller section of the store?

a) 20 wheels

b) 40 wheels

c) 60 wheels

d) 80 wheels

Unit 9
Multiply by Multiples of Ten

Standard

Number and Operations in Base Ten

Use place value understanding and properties of operations to perform multi-digit arithmetic.

3.NBT.3. Multiply one-digit whole numbers by multiples of 10 in the range 10–90 using strategies based on place value and properties of operations.

Model the Skill

Hand out ten-rods and write the following problems on the board.

$1 \times 10 = 10$ $1 \times 20 = 20$

$2 \times 10 = 20$ $2 \times 20 = 40$

◆ Have students use counters to model the first problem. **Say:** *Today we are going to look for patterns when we multiply by multiples of ten.* Demonstrate how to show 1 x 10 with base-ten blocks.

◆ **Ask:** *How many groups of tens are there? How many counters are there in the group? What is the product of 1 x 10?*

◆ **Say:** *Now let's try multiplying numbers by 20. What pattern do you see when we multiply with 20?* (Possible response: The product is the same as the fact in the tens place with a zero in the ones place.)

◆ Follow a similar process for multiplying 2 x 10 and 2 x 20.

◆ Assign students the appropriate practice page(s) to support their understanding of the skill.

Assess the Skill

Use the following problems to pre-/post-assess students' understanding of the skill.

1×20 2×20 3×20

4×20 5×20 6×20

Name _____

Use the number line. Find each product.

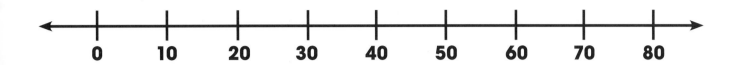

❶ 1 x 10 = _____   ❷ 0 x 20 = _____   ❸ 1 x 30 = _____

1 x 20 = _____   1 x 20 = _____   2 x 30 = _____

1 x 40 = _____   2 x 20 = _____   3 x 30 = _____

1 x 60 = _____   3 x 20 = _____   1 x 40 = _____

1 x 80 = _____   4 x 20 = _____   2 x 40 = _____

Use the number line. Find each product.

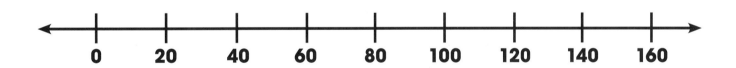

❹ 20 x 4 = _____   ❺ 3 x 20 = _____   ❻ 20 x 8 = _____

20 x 1 = _____   3 x 40 = _____   20 x 7 = _____

20 x 8 = _____   4 x 30 = _____   40 x 4 = _____

2 x 60 = _____   5 x 20 = _____   2 x 30 = _____

1 x 80 = _____   6 x 20 = _____   2 x 80 = _____

 Circle the number problems with a product of 60.

●○○   47

Name _____

Look for patterns. Then complete each table.

0   30   60   90   120   150   180   210   240

1 1 x 30 = _____   **2** 30 x 6 = _____   **3** 2 x 60 = _____

2 x 30 = _____   30 x 8 = _____   3 x 60 = _____

3 x 30 = _____   7 x 30 = _____   3 x 30 = _____

4 x 30 = _____   8 x 30 = _____   2 x 90 = _____

5 x 30 = _____   4 x 60 = _____   4 x 60 = _____

Use the number line. Find each product.

0   40   80   120   160   200   240   280   320

4 40 x 4 = _____   **5** 1 x 80 = _____   **6** 6 x 40 = _____

40 x 3 = _____   2 x 80 = _____   40 x 8 = _____

40 x 2 = _____   3 x 80 = _____   5 x 40 = _____

1 x 40 = _____   8 x 80 = _____   7 x 40 = _____

0 x 40 = _____   5 x 40 = _____   2 x 160 = _____

☆ **Tell about the patterns in the Table 8.**

Name _____

Complete the multiplication table.

x	0	1	2	3	4	5	6	7	8	9	10
0	0		0		0		0	0		0	0
10	0	10	20	30		50		70			
20	0	20	40		80						200
30	0	30		90				210		270	
40	0		80					280			
50	0	50								450	
60	0		120				360				
70	0	70		210				490			
80	0			240					640		
90	0						540				
100	0			300							1,000

☆ **Write about how this table is different from the table on page 44.**

Name _____

Solve.

1 Lara has 4 fifty-dollar bills. How much money does Lara have?

2 Jamie scored 20 points in the basketball game. Tyler scored twice that amount. How many points did Tyler score?

3 Complete the pattern in the table below.

Number of Centimeters	25	30	35	40	45	50
Number of Millimeters	250	300	350			

Circle the letter for the correct answer.

4 Julie has works 30 hours per week. How many hours does she work in 9 weeks?

a) 39 hours

b) 390 hours

c) 360 hours

d) 270 hours

5 There are 40 students riding on each bus. There are 5 buses. How many students are riding on the buses?

a) 45 students

b) 200 students

c) 20 students

d) 245 students

Unit 10
Meaning of Division

Standard

> **Operations & Algebraic Thinking**
>
> **Represent and solve problems involving multiplication and division.**
>
> **3.OA.2.** Interpret whole-number quotients of whole numbers, e.g., interpret $56 \div 8$ as the number of objects in each share when 56 objects are partitioned equally into 8 shares, or as a number of shares when 56 objects are partitioned into equal shares of 8 objects each.
>
> **Understand properties of multiplication and the relationship between multiplication and division.**
>
> **3.OA.5.** Apply properties of operations as strategies to multiply and divide.
>
> **3.OA.6.** Understand division as an unknown-factor problem.

Model the Skill

Hand out counters and write the following number sentences on the board.

$$2 + 2 + 2 = 6 \qquad 3 \times 2 = 6$$

◆ Discuss how addition and multiplication are related. **Say:** *Today we will see how subtraction and division are related.* Have students use counters to model 3 groups of 2 and model each number sentence. Then have students use counters to model repeated subtraction.

$$6 - 2 - 2 - 2 = 0 \qquad 6 \div 2 = 3$$

◆ **Ask:** *How may counters did you start with?* (6) *What number did you subtract each time?* (2) *How many times did you subtract 2? You subtracted 2 until you got an answer of 0. You subtracted 2 three times. You can say that there are 3 groups of 2 in 6.*

◆ Remind students that the answer to a division problem is called the quotient. Help students connect the repeated subtraction to the division sentence. **Ask:** *What is the quotient of $6 \div 2$?* (3)

◆ Assign students the appropriate practice page(s) to support their understanding of the skill.

Assess the Skill

Use the following problems to pre-/post-assess students' understanding of the skill.

$12 - 4 - 4 - 4 = $ _____

$12 \div 4 = $ _____

$12 - 6 - 6 = $ _____

$12 \div 6 = $ _____

Name _____

Use counters to model each subtraction. Write the missing numbers.

1 8 − 2 = _____
6 − 2 = _____
4 − 2 = _____
2 − 2 = _____

Subtract 2. Subtract 4 times.

8 ÷ 2 = _____

2 15 − 3 = _____
12 − 3 = _____
9 − 3 = _____
6 − 3 = _____
3 − 3 = _____

Subtract 3. Subtract ____ times.

15 ÷ 3 = _____

3 Subtract 2 until you get 0.
6 − 2 = _____
4 − 2 = _____
2 − 2 = _____

6 ÷ 2 = _____

4 Subtract 5 until you get 0.
20 − 5 = _____
15 − 5 = _____
10 − 5 = _____
5 − 5 = _____

20 ÷ 5 = _____

5 Subtract 3 until you get 0.
9 − 3 = _____
6 − 3 = _____
3 − 3 = _____

9 ÷ 3 = _____

6 Subtract 2 until you get 0.
14 − 2 = _____
12 − 2 = _____
10 − 2 = _____
8 − 2 = _____
6 − 2 = _____
4 − 2 = _____
2 − 2 = _____

14 ÷ 2 = _____

☆ **Tell how you got your answers.**

●○○   Unit 10 • Common Core Mathematics Grade 3 • ©2012 Newmark Learning, LLC

Name _____

Write the missing numbers.

❶

6 in all

2 equal groups

_____ in each group

6 ÷ 2 = _____

❷

12 in all

3 equal groups

_____ in each group

12 ÷ 3 = _____

❸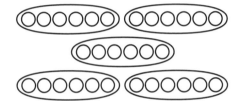

30 in all

_____ equal groups

_____ in each group

30 ÷ 5 = _____

❹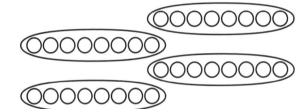

_____ in all

_____ equal groups

_____ in each group

_____ ÷ _____ = _____

❺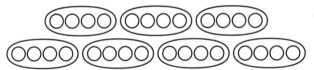

28 in all

_____ equal groups

_____ in each group

28 ÷ 7 = _____

❻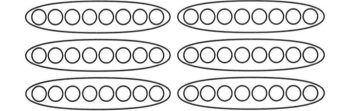

_____ in all

_____ equal groups

_____ in each group

_____ ÷ _____ = _____

☆ **Tell what each number in the division sentence means.**

Name _____

**Use counters to model the problem. Draw rings to show the groups.
Write the missing numbers.**

1 4 in each group
_____ equal groups

$8 \div 4 =$ _____

2 4 in each group
_____ equal groups

$12 \div 3 =$ _____

3 2 in each group
_____ equal groups

$12 \div 2 =$ _____

4 3 in each group
_____ equal groups

$15 \div 3 =$ _____

5 3 equal groups
_____ in each group

$6 \div 3 =$ _____

6 3 equal groups
_____ in each group

$21 \div 3 =$ _____

7 2 equal groups
_____ in each group

$10 \div 2 =$ _____

8 4 equal groups
_____ in each group

$16 \div 4 =$ _____

☆ **Tell how you solved each problem.**

Name _____

Solve.

1 We have 48 slices of pizza. Each whole pizza has eight slices. How many whole pizzas do we have?

2 Jon has 3 equal rows of lemon trees. He has 27 lemon trees in all. How many trees does he have in each row?

3 The lake is 24 miles away. If we bike at 8 miles per hour, how long will it take to get to the lake?

4 There are 32 horseshoes in the barn. If each horse needs 4 horseshoes, how many horses can get new shoes?

Circle the letter for the correct answer.

5 Zach has 63 pages left in his book. If he reads 9 pages a day, how many days will it take him to finish his book?

a) 9 days

b) 8 days

c) 7 days

d) 6 days

6 The theater has 320 seats. There are 8 rows of seats. Which division sentence shows how many seats are in each row?

a) 8 x 40 = 320 seats

b) 320 x 8 = 40 seats

c) 320 ÷ 40 = 8 seats

d) 320 ÷ 8 = 40 seats

Unit 11
Fact Families for Multiplication and Division

Standard

Operations & Algebraic Thinking

Multiply and divide within 100.

3.OA.7. Fluently multiply and divide within 100, using strategies such as the relationship between multiplication and division or properties of operations. By the end of Grade 3, know from memory all products of two one-digit numbers.

Model the Skill

Hand out counters and write the following problems on the board.

$$3 \times 4 = 12$$
$$12 \div 3 = 4$$

◆ **Say:** *Multiplication and division are opposite operations. That means they undo each other.* Demonstrate how to use counters to model 3 groups of 4. **Ask:** *How many groups of counters are there? (3) How many counters are in each group? (4) How many counters are there in all? (12)*

◆ Then demonstrate how to separate 12 counters into 3 equal groups. **Ask:** *How many counters did I start with? (12) How many groups did I make? (3) How many counters are there in each group? (4)* **Say:** *12 divided into 3 groups is 4 in each group.* Remind students that the answer to a division problem is called the quotient. Demonstrate how to record the quotient.

◆ Assign students the appropriate practice page(s) to support their understanding of the skill.

Assess the Skill

Use the following problems to pre-/post-assess students' understanding of the skill. Ask students to complete the following fact families.

$5 \times 6 = 30$ $\qquad\qquad\qquad$ $4 \times 9 = 36$

_____ X _____ = _____ $\qquad$ _____ X _____ = _____

_____ ÷ _____ = _____ $\qquad$ _____ ÷ _____ = _____

_____ ÷ _____ = _____ $\qquad$ _____ ÷ _____ = _____

Find the missing numbers.

❶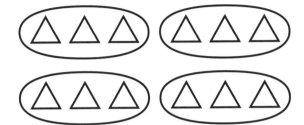

$4 \times 3 = 12$

$12 \div 4 = $ _____

_____ x _____ = _____

_____ ÷ _____ = _____

❷

$5 \times 6 = 30$

$30 \div 5 = $ _____

_____ x _____ = _____

_____ ÷ _____ = _____

Match the multiplication sentence to the related division sentence. Then solve.

❸ $3 \times 5 = 15$ $32 \div 4 = $ _____

❹ $4 \times 8 = 32$ $35 \div 7 = $ _____

❺ $7 \times 5 = 35$ $8 \div 4 = $ _____

❻ $4 \times 2 = 8$ $15 \div 3 = $ _____

☆   **Tell how you got your answers.**

Name _____

Use counters. Complete each fact family.

1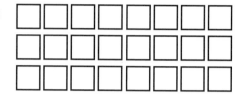

5 x 4 = 20

4 x 5 = _____

20 ÷ 5 = _____

20 ÷ 4 = _____

2

3 x 8 = 24

8 x 3 = _____

24 ÷ 8 = _____

24 ÷ 3 = _____

---

3 7 x 2 = 14

____ x ____ = ____

____ ÷ ____ = ____

____ ÷ ____ = ____

4 3 x 6 = 18

____ x ____ = ____

____ ÷ ____ = ____

____ ÷ ____ = ____

5 4 x 6 = 24

____ x ____ = ____

____ ÷ ____ = ____

____ ÷ ____ = ____

---

6 5 x 7 = 35

____ x ____ = ____

____ ÷ ____ = ____

____ ÷ ____ = ____

7 7 x 9 = 63

____ x ____ = ____

____ ÷ ____ = ____

____ ÷ ____ = ____

8 6 x 9 = 54

____ x ____ = ____

____ ÷ ____ = ____

____ ÷ ____ = ____

☆ **Tell how you found the missing numbers.**

Name _____

Complete each fact family.

1 2 x 9 = 18

  9 x 2 = _____

  18 ÷ 2 = _____

  18 ÷ 9 = _____

2 3 x 8 = 24

  8 x 3 = _____

  24 ÷ 3 = _____

  24 ÷ 8 = _____

3 4 x 7 = 28

  7 x 4 = _____

  28 ÷ 7 = _____

  28 ÷ 4 = _____

4 7 x 5 = 35

  5 x 7 = _____

  35 ÷ 7 = _____

  35 ÷ 5 = _____

5 9 x 4 = 36

  4 x 9 = _____

  36 ÷ 9 = _____

  36 ÷ 4 = _____

6 6 x 8 = 48

  8 x 6 = _____

  48 ÷ 8 = _____

  48 ÷ 6 = _____

Use the numbers to write a fact family.

7 5, 6, 30

  ___ x ___ = ___

  ___ x ___ = ___

  ___ ÷ ___ = ___

  ___ ÷ ___ = ___

8 9, 3, 27

  ___ x ___ = ___

  ___ x ___ = ___

  ___ ÷ ___ = ___

  ___ ÷ ___ = ___

9 4, 6, 24

  ___ x ___ = ___

  ___ x ___ = ___

  ___ ÷ ___ = ___

  ___ ÷ ___ = ___

10 3, 7, 21

  ___ x ___ = ___

  ___ x ___ = ___

  ___ ÷ ___ = ___

  ___ ÷ ___ = ___

11 4, 8, 32

  ___ x ___ = ___

  ___ x ___ = ___

  ___ ÷ ___ = ___

  ___ ÷ ___ = ___

12 2, 8, 16

  ___ x ___ = ___

  ___ x ___ = ___

  ___ ÷ ___ = ___

  ___ ÷ ___ = ___

● ● ●

Name _____

Solve.

1 We have 42 oranges in 7 equal bags. How many oranges are in each bag?

2 Each basket has 8 pears. We have 32 pears. How many baskets of pears do we have?

3 Each bunch has 6 bananas. We have 42 bananas. How many bunches do we have?

4 Marissa baked 4 apple pies. She used 8 apples in each pie. How many apples did she use?

Circle the letter for the correct answer.

5 Which number sentence completes the fact family below?

$$7 \times 3 = 21$$
$$3 \times 7 = 21$$
$$21 \div 7 = 3$$

a) $3 \times 7 = 21$

b) $27 \div 7 = 9$

c) $21 \div 3 = 7$

d) $7 \div 3 = 21$

6 Which of the following number sentences is not part of the fact family for 4, 6, and 24?

a) $4 \times 6 = 24$

b) $24 \div 6 = 4$

c) $24 \div 4 = 6$

d) $26 \div 4 = 4$

Unit 12
Solve Multiplication and Division Problems

Standard

Operations & Algebraic Thinking

Represent and solve problems involving multiplication and division.

3.OA.3. Use multiplication and division within 100 to solve word problems in situations involving equal groups, arrays, and measurement quantities, e.g., by using drawings and equations with a symbol for the unknown number to represent the problem.

Model the Skill

Hand out counters and write the following problem on the board.

There are 3 flowers in each vase. There are 5 vases. How many flowers are there?

◆ **Say:** *Today we are going to solve different types of word problems. Look at the problem. How many flowers are there in each vase? (3) How many vases are there? (5) There are 5 groups of 3 flowers. How can we find how many flowers there are in all?* Have students share different strategies for finding the total number of flowers. (15; Possible responses: count the flowers; find the total of 5 groups of 3)

◆ Use counters to demonstrate how to use repeated addition or multiplication to solve the problem. **Say:** *You can use repeated addition or multiplication to find the total number of flowers. The sum and the product will be the same.*

◆ Assign students the appropriate practice page(s) to support their understanding of the skill.

Assess the Skill

Use the following problems to pre-/post-assess students' understanding of the skill.

$5 \times 6 = 30$ $4 \times 9 = 36$

_____ X _____ = _____   _____ X _____ = _____

_____ ÷ _____ = _____   _____ X _____ = _____

_____ ÷ _____ = _____   _____ X _____ = _____

Name _____

Solve each problem.

1 There are 3 flowers in each vase. There are 6 vases. How many flowers are there?

_____ flowers

2 There are 8 crayons in each box. There are 5 boxes of crayons. How many crayons are there?

_____ crayons

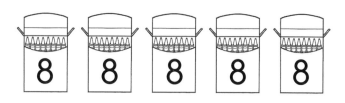

3 There are 4 rows of flowers. There are 3 flowers in each row. How many flowers are there?

_____ flowers

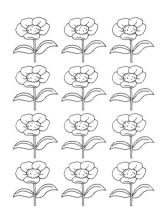

4 There are 4 rows of apples. There are 8 apples in each row. How many apples are there?

_____ apples

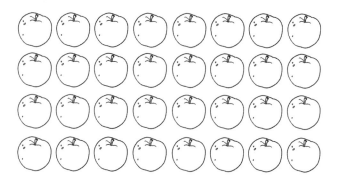

☆ **Tell how you got your answers.**

●○○

Solve each problem.

1 Sam has 15 apples. He places an equal number of apples on each plate. He has 3 plates. How many apples does he put on each plate?

_____ apples

2 Lisa has 5 row of flowers. There are 5 flowers in each row. How many flowers are there?

_____ flowers

3 Tim is digging holes to plant seeds. Tim has 32 seeds. He puts 4 seeds in each hole. How many holes does he dig?

_____ holes

4 Jane is making 2 peach pies. She puts 8 peaches in each pie. How many peaches does she need?

_____ peaches

5 Piper has 16 slices of cheese. She puts 4 slices on each sandwich. How many sandwiches can she make?

_____ sandwiches

6 Ryan has 21 carrots. He puts 7 carrots in each basket. How many baskets does he need?

_____ baskets

☆ **Tell how you got your answers.**

Name _____

Draw and array to solve each problem.

1 There are 3 rows of chairs. There are 5 chairs in each row. How many chairs are there?

_____ chairs

2 There are 8 rows of flowers. There are 6 flowers in each row. How many flowers are there?

_____ flowers

3 There are 18 roses. There are 6 in each vase. How many vases are there?

_____ vases

4 There are 6 rows of cookies. There are 7 cookies in each row. How many cookies are there?

_____ cookies

5 There are 24 plants in the garden. There are 4 plants in each row. How many rows of plants are there?

_____ rows

6 There are 4 benches in the park. Each bench has 6 seats. How many seats are there?

_____ seats

7 Mike plants 45 seeds in equal rows. He plants 9 seeds in each row. How many rows does he plant?

_____ rows

8 David has 36 marbles. He wants to put 9 marbles in each bag. How many bags does he use?

_____ bags

 Tell how you know your answer is reasonable.

●●●

Name _____

Solve.

1 Elena has 8 pairs of shoes. How many shoes does she have in all?

2 Anita bakes 36 muffins. She put 9 muffins in each pan. How many pans of muffins did she make?

3 Dan builds a wall with blocks. He puts 6 blocks in each row. He builds 9 rows. How many blocks does he use?

4 Marco picked 42 apples. He put them in 6 baskets. He put the same number of apples in each basket. How many apples did he put in each basket?

Circle the letter for the correct answer.

5 Lil has 4 pens. She has 5 times as many crayons. How many crayons does she have?

a) 5 crayons

b) 9 crayons

c) 16 crayons

d) 20 crayons

6 Dominic has 72 rocks in his collection. He keeps them in one full case with 8 rocks in each row. How many rows are in the case?

a) 90 rocks

b) 9 rows

c) 7 rocks

d) 7 rows

Unit 13
Use Multiplication or Division to Find the Missing Number

Standard

Operations & Algebraic Thinking

Represent and solve problems involving multiplication and division.

3.OA.4. Determine the unknown whole number in a multiplication or division equation relating three whole numbers.

Understand properties of multiplication and the relationship between multiplication and division.

3.OA.6. Understand division as an unknown-factor problem.

Model the Skill

Hand out counters and write the following problem on the board.

$$4 \times 6 = \underline{\hspace{1.5cm}}$$

◆ **Say:** *Today we are going to model multiplication problems to find the missing product or factor.* Remind students that the factors are the numbers that are multiplied, and the product is the answer to the multiplication problem.

◆ Have students look at the problem above. **Ask:** *Is the product or a factor missing?* (product) *How do you know?* (Possible answer: The missing number is by itself after the equal sign.) *What are the factors?* (4 and 6) *How can you model the problem?* (Possible response: Show 4 groups of 6 counters.) Have students model, record, and share their work. **Ask:** *What is the product?* (24)

$$4 \times \underline{\hspace{1.5cm}} = 24$$

◆ Write the above follow-up problem on the board, and have students look at it. **Ask:** *Is the product or a factor missing?* (factor) *How do you know?* (Possible answer: The missing number comes right after the multiplication sign.) Have students model the problem with counters, then draw to record their work.

◆ Assign students the appropriate practice page(s) to support their understanding of the skill. Have them share their strategies for finding the missing numbers in the problems.

Assess the Skill

Use the following problems to pre-/post-assess students' understanding of the skill.

$$4 \times 6 = \underline{\hspace{1.5cm}} \qquad\qquad 32 \div \underline{\hspace{1.5cm}} = 8$$

$$25 \div \underline{\hspace{1.5cm}} = 5 \qquad\qquad \underline{\hspace{1.5cm}} \div 7 = 3$$

Name _____

Complete each number sentence.

❶

2 x 3 = _____

❷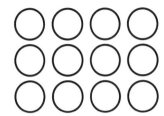

3 x 4 = _____

❸

8 x 3 = _____

❹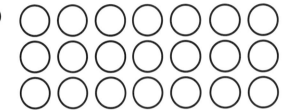

3 x _____ = 21

❺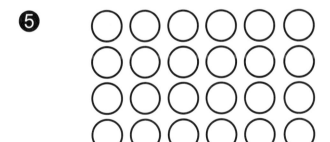

_____ x 6 = 24

❻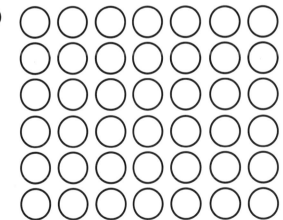

7 x _____ = 42

 Tell how to use your picture to solve the problem.

●○○   67

Use counters to model the problem. Draw a picture to show your work. Complete each number sentence.

1

$15 \div 5 =$ _____

2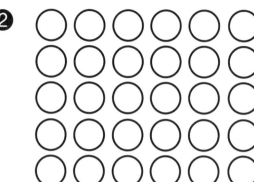

_____ $\div 6 = 5$

3

$9 \times$ _____ $= 72$

4

$16 \div$ _____ $= 4$

5

$49 \div$ _____ $= 7$

6

$48 \div$ _____ $= 8$

7

$36 \div$ _____ $= 4$

8

$54 \div$ _____ $= 9$

 Tell how you solved the problem.

Name _____

Use an array to solve each problem.

1 8 ÷ 4 = _____

2 6 x _____ = 18

3 _____ x 8 = 40

4 12 ÷ 3 = _____

5 6 x 5 = _____

6 4 x _____ = 16

7 _____ x 5 = 20

8 27 ÷ 3 = _____

9 _____ x 9 = 36

10 42 ÷ 6 = _____

11 _____ x 8 = 48

12 63 ÷ 7 = _____

 Tell how you solved each problem.

Solve.

1 Angelo has 18 black socks. How many pairs of black socks does he have in all?

2 Dad has 27 turnip plants in the garden. He has them in 3 equal rows. How many turnip plants are in each row?

3 Brittany has 24 apples. She puts an equal number of apples in 6 tarts? How many apples are in each tart?

4 Mom has 54 dollars. She spends it all on sandwiches for the party. Each sandwich is 6 dollars. How many sandwiches does she buy?

Circle the letter for the correct answer.

5 Mr. Gomez has to make 30 3-page packets. Each packet requires 1 staple. How many pages of paper and how many staples does he need?

a) 33 pages and 33 staples

b) 30 pages and 30 staples

c) 10 pages and 10 staples

d) 90 pages and 30 staples

6 Hudson has 2 full reels of fishing line. He has a total of 20 yards of line. There are 3 feet in a yard. How many feet of fishing line are on each reel?

a) 120 feet

b) 60 feet

c) 30 feet

d) 25 feet

Unit 14
Understand Fractions

Standard

> **Number & Operations—Fractions**
>
> **Develop understanding of fractions as numbers.**
>
> **3.NF.1.** Understand a fraction *1/b* as the quantity formed by 1 part when a whole is partitioned into *b* equal parts; understand a fraction *a/b* as the quantity formed by *a* parts of size *1/b*.

Model the Skill

Draw the following figure on the board.

◆ **Say:** *Today we are going to learn about fractions. A fraction names part of a whole or part of a group. Look at this rectangle. How many equal parts is the rectangle divided into?* (2) *Each part is one-half of the whole rectangle.*

◆ Write the fraction $\frac{1}{2}$ on the board. Have students look at the fraction $\frac{1}{2}$ and point to the numerator. **Say:** *The numerator is the top number of a fraction. The numerator names a part of the whole.* Have students point to the denominator. **Say:** *The denominator is the bottom number of a fraction. The denominator tells how many equal parts are in the whole.*

◆ Model writing the fraction for the rectangle again. **Ask:** *How many equal parts are in the whole rectangle?* (2) *What fraction names each equal share or part?* ($\frac{1}{2}$) Have students practice writing the fraction for similar shapes sectioned in halves, thirds, and fourths or quarters.

◆ Assign students the appropriate practice page(s) to support their understanding of the skill and share their strategies for finding the missing numbers in each fraction. They should recognize that the denominator is always the same as the number of equal parts. Have them identify whether the numerator or the denominator is the missing number.

Assess the Skill

Use the following problems to pre-/post-assess students' understanding of the skill.

◆ **Ask:** *How many equal parts are in the whole? How many equal parts are shaded? What fraction shows the shaded part?*

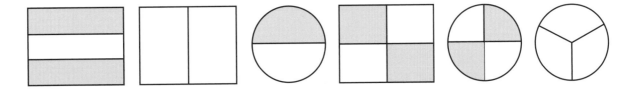

Name _____

Write each missing number.

1

_____ equal parts

Each part is $\frac{1}{2}$.

2

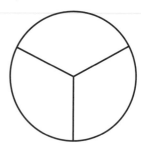

_____ equal parts

Each part is $\frac{\square}{3}$.

3

_____ equal parts

Each part is $\frac{1}{\square}$.

4

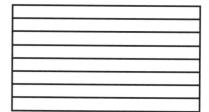

_____ equal parts

Each part is $\frac{1}{\square}$.

5

_____ equal parts

Each part is $\frac{1}{\square}$.

6

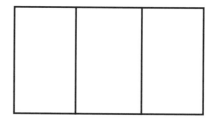

_____ equal parts

Each part is $\frac{1}{\square}$.

 Tell how you found the missing numbers.

Match the picture with the fraction that names the shaded part.

❶

$\dfrac{1}{2}$

❷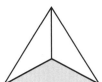

$\dfrac{1}{8}$

❸

$\dfrac{2}{8}$

❹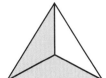

$\dfrac{1}{3}$

❺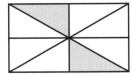

$\dfrac{1}{2}$

❻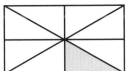

$\dfrac{1}{4}$

❼

$\dfrac{2}{4}$

❽

$\dfrac{2}{3}$

 Tell how you made each match.

Name _____

Write the missing numbers.

1 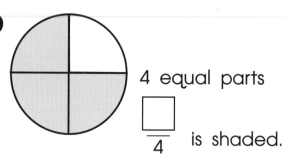   4 equal parts

$\dfrac{\boxed{}}{4}$ is shaded.

2 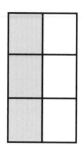   6 equal parts

$\dfrac{\boxed{}}{6}$ is shaded.

3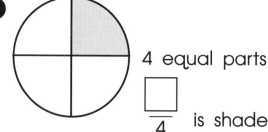

_____ equal parts

$\dfrac{\boxed{}}{\boxed{}}$ is shaded.

4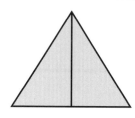

_____ equal parts

$\dfrac{\boxed{}}{\boxed{}}$ is shaded.

5 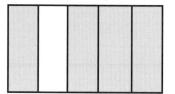   4 equal parts

$\dfrac{\boxed{}}{4}$ is shaded.

6 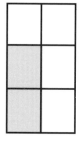   6 equal parts

$\dfrac{\boxed{}}{6}$ is shaded.

7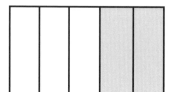

_____ equal parts

$\dfrac{\boxed{}}{\boxed{}}$ is shaded.

8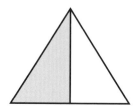

_____ equal parts

$\dfrac{\boxed{}}{\boxed{}}$ is shaded.

☆ **Tell how you found the missing numbers.**

Name _____

Solve.

1 We cut the grapefruit in 2 equal pieces. I ate 1 piece. How much did I eat?

2 We have 3 kittens. 2 kittens have stripes and 1 kitten has spots. What fraction of the kittens has spots?

3 Sloane has 4 cards in her hand. 3 cards are red. The rest are black. What fraction of the cards is red?

4 A pizza has 8 slices. 3 slices have olives. What fraction of the pizza has olives?

Circle the letter for the correct answer.

5 The book has 8 pages. 5 pages have pictures. What fraction of the book's pages has pictures?

a) $\frac{1}{8}$

b) $\frac{1}{5}$

c) $\frac{8}{5}$

d) $\frac{5}{8}$

6 Austin's room has 3 lights. 2 of the lights are on. 1 of the lights is off. What fraction of the lights in Austin's room is on?

a) $\frac{1}{2}$

b) $\frac{1}{3}$

c) $\frac{2}{2}$

d) $\frac{2}{3}$

Unit 15
Fractions on a Number Line

Number & Operations—Fractions

Develop understanding of fractions as numbers.

3.NF.2. Understand a fraction as a number on the number line; represent fractions on a number line diagram.

a) Represent a fraction *1/b* on a number line diagram by defining the interval from 0 to 1 as the whole and partitioning it into *b* equal parts. Recognize that each part has size *1/b* and that the endpoint of the part based at 0 locates the number *1/b* on the number line.

b) Represent a fraction *a/b* on a number line diagram by marking off *a* lengths *1/b* from 0. Recognize that the resulting interval has size *a/b* and that its endpoint locates the number *a/b* on the number line.

Model the Skill

Draw the following number line.

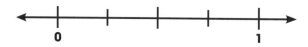

◆ **Say:** *You can use a number line to show fractions. Look at this number line. How does the number line show equal parts?* (Possible response: The tick marks are spaced equally.) *How many equal spaces are there?* Help students count each equal part of the number line to verify that there are 4 equal parts.

◆ Point out the 0 and 1 under the first and last tick marks. **Say:** *The number line shows one whole. Each space is one equal part of the number line. Since this number line is divided into 4 equal spaces, we can say that it shows fourths, or quarters.*

◆ Add tick marks to show eighths. **Ask:** *Now how many equal parts does this number line have? Which word tells how this number line is divided?* (eighths)

◆ Assign students the appropriate practice page(s) to support their understanding of the skill.

Assess the Skill

Use the following problems to pre-/post-assess students' understanding of the skill.

◆ Have students label the number line with the following points:

$\frac{1}{2}$, $\frac{1}{4}$, and $\frac{1}{8}$

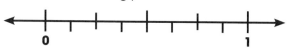

Name _____

Match each number line to the equal parts it shows.

1

fourths

2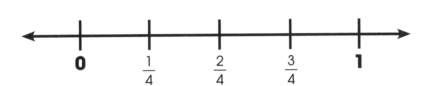

eighths

3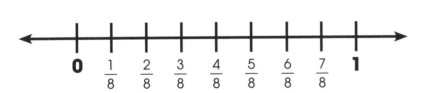

sixths

4

halves

5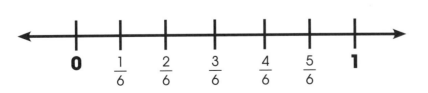

thirds

 Tell how you know the number line matches the equal parts.

Name _____

Draw a point on each number line to show the fraction.

❶ $\dfrac{1}{2}$

$\dfrac{0}{2}$ ⟷————|————|————|———→ $\dfrac{2}{2}$
0   1

❷ $\dfrac{1}{8}$

$\dfrac{0}{8}$ $\dfrac{2}{8}$ $\dfrac{4}{8}$ $\dfrac{5}{8}$ $\dfrac{6}{8}$ $\dfrac{7}{8}$

0   1

❸ $\dfrac{1}{4}$

$\dfrac{0}{4}$ $\dfrac{2}{4}$

0   1

❹ $\dfrac{1}{6}$

$\dfrac{0}{6}$ $\dfrac{3}{6}$

0   1

❺ $\dfrac{1}{3}$

0   1

❻ $\dfrac{3}{8}$

$\dfrac{0}{8}$ $\dfrac{2}{8}$ $\dfrac{4}{8}$ $\dfrac{5}{8}$ $\dfrac{6}{8}$ $\dfrac{7}{8}$

0   1

❼ $\dfrac{3}{4}$

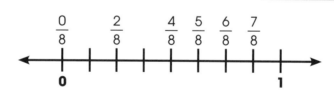

$\dfrac{0}{4}$ $\dfrac{2}{4}$

0   1

❽ $\dfrac{5}{6}$

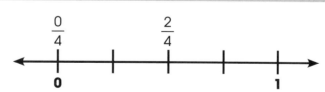

$\dfrac{0}{6}$ $\dfrac{3}{6}$

0   1

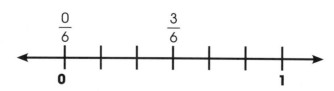

 Tell how you know the fraction matches the point on the number line.

Name _____

Write a fraction that names each point.

1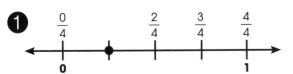

2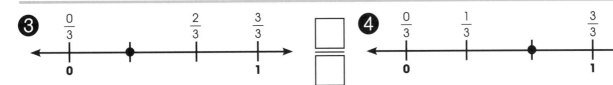

3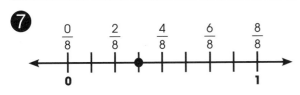

4

5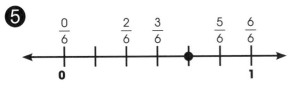

6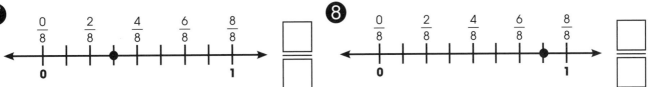

7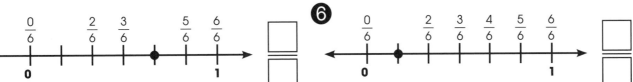

8

9

10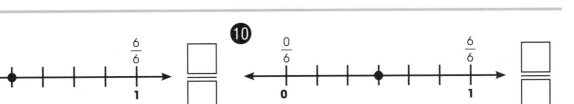

11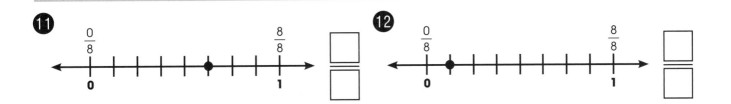

12

 Tell how you found the fraction to name the point on the number line.

Name _____

Solve.

1 Complete the number line.

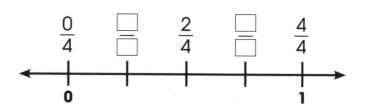

2 Complete the number line.

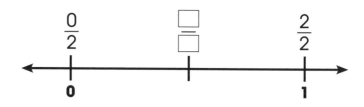

3 Complete the number line.

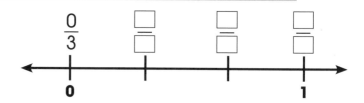

Circle the letter for the correct answer.

4 Which number line shows $\frac{7}{8}$?

a)

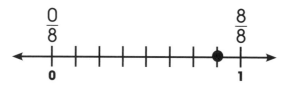

b)

c)

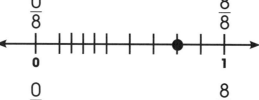

Unit 16
Equivalent Fractions

Standard

Number & Operations—Fractions

Develop understanding of fractions as numbers.

3.NF.3. Explain equivalence of fractions in special cases, and compare fractions by reasoning about their size.
   a) Understand two fractions as equivalent (equal) if they are the same size, or the same point on a number line.
   b) Recognize and generate simple equivalent fractions, e.g., 1/2 = 2/4, 4/6 = 2/3). Explain why the fractions are equivalent, e.g., by using a visual fraction model.
   c) Express whole numbers as fractions, and recognize fractions that are equivalent to whole numbers.

Model the Skill

Hand out fraction bars and draw the following model on the board.

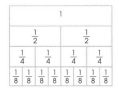

◆ **Say:** *Today we are going to learn about equivalent fractions. Equivalent fractions are fractions that are equal—they name the same amount.* Have students use fraction bars to model one-half. **Say:** *We want to see how many fourths it takes to equal one-half.* Have students use fraction bars to model the fourths.

◆ **Ask:** *How many fourths are equal to one-half? How do you know?* (2. It takes two-fourths to be the same size as one-half.) **Say:** *One-half and two-fourths are the same size. One-half and two-fourths are equivalent fractions.* You might suggest that students place the fourths on top of the half as another way to show they are equal.

◆ Assign students the appropriate practice page(s) to support their understanding of the skill.

Assess the Skill

Use the following problems to pre-/post-assess students' understanding of the skill.

$\frac{1}{2} = \frac{\square}{4}$ $\qquad$ $\frac{1}{2} = \frac{\square}{6}$ $\qquad$ $\frac{1}{2} = \frac{\square}{8}$ $\qquad$ $\frac{1}{2} = \frac{\square}{10}$

$\frac{3}{6} = \frac{\square}{2}$ $\qquad$ $\frac{3}{4} = \frac{\square}{8}$ $\qquad$ $\frac{1}{4} = \frac{\square}{8}$ $\qquad$ $\frac{2}{4} = \frac{\square}{2}$

Name _____

Use fraction bars or a number line. Write the missing numerator.

1

$\frac{1}{2}$	
$\frac{1}{4}$	$\frac{1}{4}$

$$\frac{1}{2} \;=\; \frac{\Box}{4}$$

2

$\frac{1}{4}$

$\frac{1}{8}$	$\frac{1}{8}$

$$\frac{1}{4} \;=\; \frac{\Box}{8}$$

3

$\frac{1}{3}$

$\frac{1}{6}$	$\frac{1}{6}$

$$\frac{1}{3} \;=\; \frac{\Box}{6}$$

4

$\frac{1}{4}$	$\frac{1}{4}$

$\frac{1}{8}$	$\frac{1}{8}$	$\frac{1}{8}$	$\frac{1}{8}$

$$\frac{2}{4} \;=\; \frac{\Box}{8}$$

5

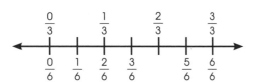

$$\frac{2}{3} \;=\; \frac{\Box}{6}$$

6

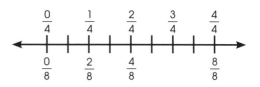

$$\frac{3}{4} \;=\; \frac{\Box}{8}$$

☆ **Circle the fractions that are equivalent to one-half.**

● ○ ○

Use fraction bars or a number line. Write equivalent fractions.

1	
$\frac{1}{2}$	$\frac{1}{2}$

$\frac{1}{4}$	$\frac{1}{4}$	$\frac{1}{4}$	$\frac{1}{4}$

| $\frac{1}{8}$ | $\frac{1}{8}$ | $\frac{1}{8}$ | $\frac{1}{8}$ | $\frac{1}{8}$ | $\frac{1}{8}$ | $\frac{1}{8}$ | $\frac{1}{8}$ |

1		
$\frac{1}{3}$	$\frac{1}{3}$	$\frac{1}{3}$

| $\frac{1}{6}$ | $\frac{1}{6}$ | $\frac{1}{6}$ | $\frac{1}{6}$ | $\frac{1}{6}$ | $\frac{1}{6}$ |

1	
$\frac{1}{2}$	$\frac{1}{2}$

| $\frac{1}{5}$ | $\frac{1}{5}$ | $\frac{1}{5}$ | $\frac{1}{5}$ | $\frac{1}{5}$ |

| $\frac{1}{10}$ | $\frac{1}{10}$ | $\frac{1}{10}$ | $\frac{1}{10}$ | $\frac{1}{10}$ | $\frac{1}{10}$ | $\frac{1}{10}$ | $\frac{1}{10}$ | $\frac{1}{10}$ | $\frac{1}{10}$ |

1 $\frac{1}{3} = \dfrac{\square}{\square}$

2 $\frac{2}{3} = \dfrac{\square}{\square}$

3 $\frac{3}{3} = \dfrac{\square}{\square}$

4 $\frac{1}{2} = \dfrac{\square}{\square}$

5 $\frac{1}{4} = \dfrac{\square}{\square}$

6 $\frac{3}{4} = \dfrac{\square}{\square}$

7 $\frac{2}{8} = \dfrac{\square}{\square}$

8 $\frac{4}{8} = \dfrac{\square}{\square}$

9 $\frac{6}{8} = \dfrac{\square}{\square}$

10 $\frac{2}{10} = \dfrac{\square}{\square}$

11 $\frac{4}{10} = \dfrac{\square}{\square}$

12 $\frac{6}{10} = \dfrac{\square}{\square}$

 Tell how you know the fractions are equivalent.

Name _____

Use fraction bars or a number line. Write equivalent fractions.

1 $\dfrac{2}{3}$ = $\dfrac{\square}{\square}$

2 $\dfrac{1}{4}$ = $\dfrac{\square}{\square}$

3 $\dfrac{2}{5}$ = $\dfrac{\square}{\square}$

4 $\dfrac{3}{6}$ = $\dfrac{\square}{\square}$

5 $\dfrac{4}{4}$ = $\dfrac{\square}{\square}$

6 $\dfrac{6}{8}$ = $\dfrac{\square}{\square}$

7 $\dfrac{2}{5}$ = $\dfrac{\square}{\square}$

8 $\dfrac{4}{8}$ = $\dfrac{\square}{\square}$

9 $\dfrac{6}{6}$ = $\dfrac{\square}{\square}$

10 $\dfrac{6}{10}$ = $\dfrac{\square}{\square}$

11 $\dfrac{4}{6}$ = $\dfrac{\square}{\square}$

12 $\dfrac{5}{10}$ = $\dfrac{\square}{\square}$

13 $\dfrac{2}{8}$ = $\dfrac{\square}{\square}$

14 $\dfrac{1}{3}$ = $\dfrac{\square}{\square}$

15 $\dfrac{4}{5}$ = $\dfrac{\square}{\square}$

☆ **Explain how you find equivalent fractions.**

Name _____

Solve.

1 A pizza has 8 slices. One-half of the pizza has meatballs. How many slices have meatballs?

$$\frac{1}{2} = \frac{?}{8}$$

2 The fruit bowl has 6 apples. Half of the apples are green. How many apples are green?

$$\frac{1}{2} = \frac{?}{6}$$

3 Robin has some bananas. 6 bananas are ripe. Three-fifths of the bananas are ripe. How many bananas does Robin have in all?

$$\frac{3}{5} = \frac{6}{?}$$

4 Tate has 4 dollars in her wallet. One-half of her dollars are in her wallet. How many dollars does she have in all?

$$\frac{1}{2} = \frac{4}{?}$$

5 Which of the following fractions is equal to one-half?

a) $\frac{4}{6}$

b) $\frac{2}{3}$

c) $\frac{4}{2}$

d) $\frac{2}{4}$

6 Nils has 9 pages in the chapter. He has read 3 pages. How much of the chapter has he read?

a) $\frac{9}{3}$

b) $\frac{1}{2}$

c) $\frac{1}{4}$

d) $\frac{1}{3}$

Unit 17
Compare Fractions

Standard

Number & Operations—Fractions

Develop understanding of fractions as numbers.

3.NF.3. d) Compare two fractions with the same numerator or the same denominator by reasoning about their size. Recognize that comparisons are valid only when the two fractions refer to the same whole. Record the results of comparisons with the symbols >, =, or <, and justify the conclusions, e.g., by using a visual fraction model.

Model the Skill

Hand out fraction bars.

◆ Remind students how they can use symbols to compare whole numbers. Review the meaning of the symbols <, >, and =. **Say:** *Today we are going to use symbols to compare fractions.* Have students use fraction bars to model the problem. **Say:** *When the denominators are the same, the fraction with the greater numerator is the greater fraction.* **Ask:** *Which is greater, $\frac{1}{3}$ or $\frac{2}{3}$?* ($\frac{2}{3}$) *How do you know?* (Possible response: When you look at the models, $\frac{2}{3}$ is larger than $\frac{1}{3}$.) **Say:** *$\frac{2}{3}$ is greater than $\frac{1}{3}$. Another way to say this is $\frac{1}{3}$ is less than $\frac{2}{3}$. What symbol will you write in the circle?* ("is less than" symbol) *$\frac{1}{3}$ is less than $\frac{2}{3}$.*

◆ Assign students the appropriate practice page(s) to support their understanding of the skill. Point out that when fractions in a pair have the same numerator and denominator, they are equal. **Say:** *$\frac{3}{8}$ is equal to $\frac{3}{8}$. Is $\frac{3}{3}$ = $\frac{6}{6}$?* Discuss why.

Assess the Skill

Use the following problems to pre-/post-assess students' understanding of the skill.

$$\frac{2}{8} \bigcirc \frac{5}{8} \qquad \frac{1}{8} \bigcirc \frac{1}{2} \qquad \frac{3}{6} < \frac{\square}{6}$$

$$\frac{2}{4} \bigcirc \frac{1}{3} \qquad \frac{4}{4} \bigcirc \frac{3}{3} \qquad \frac{3}{4} > \frac{\square}{4}$$

Name _____

Use fraction bars. Compare the fractions. Write <, >, or =.

1 $\frac{1}{3}$ ◯ $\frac{2}{3}$

$\frac{1}{3}$	

$\frac{1}{3}$	$\frac{1}{3}$

2 $\frac{4}{6}$ ◯ $\frac{3}{6}$

$\frac{1}{6}$	$\frac{1}{6}$	$\frac{1}{6}$	$\frac{1}{6}$

$\frac{1}{6}$	$\frac{1}{6}$	$\frac{1}{6}$

---

3 $\frac{2}{8}$ ◯ $\frac{5}{8}$

$\frac{1}{8}$	$\frac{1}{8}$

$\frac{1}{8}$	$\frac{1}{8}$	$\frac{1}{8}$	$\frac{1}{8}$	$\frac{1}{8}$

4 $\frac{2}{5}$ ◯ $\frac{4}{5}$

$\frac{1}{5}$	$\frac{1}{5}$

$\frac{1}{5}$	$\frac{1}{5}$	$\frac{1}{5}$	$\frac{1}{5}$

---

5 $\frac{2}{10}$ ◯ $\frac{4}{10}$

$\frac{1}{10}$	$\frac{1}{10}$

$\frac{1}{10}$	$\frac{1}{10}$	$\frac{1}{10}$	$\frac{1}{10}$

6 $\frac{5}{5}$ ◯ $\frac{2}{5}$

$\frac{1}{5}$	$\frac{1}{5}$	$\frac{1}{5}$	$\frac{1}{5}$	$\frac{1}{5}$

$\frac{1}{5}$	$\frac{1}{5}$

---

7 $\frac{1}{4}$ ◯ $\frac{1}{2}$

$\frac{1}{4}$	$\frac{1}{4}$	$\frac{1}{4}$	$\frac{1}{4}$

$\frac{1}{2}$	$\frac{1}{2}$

8 $\frac{6}{6}$ ◯ $\frac{3}{3}$

$\frac{1}{6}$	$\frac{1}{6}$	$\frac{1}{6}$	$\frac{1}{6}$	$\frac{1}{6}$	$\frac{1}{6}$

$\frac{1}{3}$	$\frac{1}{3}$	$\frac{1}{3}$

 Look at the page. Draw a circle around the fractions that show fifths.

Name _____

Use fraction bars. Compare the fractions. Write <, >, or =.

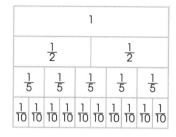

1 $\frac{1}{2}$ ◯ $\frac{1}{4}$

2 $\frac{1}{6}$ ◯ $\frac{1}{3}$

3 $\frac{2}{4}$ ◯ $\frac{4}{4}$

4 $\frac{2}{5}$ ◯ $\frac{2}{6}$

5 $\frac{5}{6}$ ◯ $\frac{2}{6}$

6 $\frac{2}{4}$ ◯ $\frac{3}{4}$

7 $\frac{3}{6}$ ◯ $\frac{3}{3}$

8 $\frac{2}{5}$ ◯ $\frac{2}{10}$

9 $\frac{3}{8}$ ◯ $\frac{7}{8}$

10 $\frac{4}{10}$ ◯ $\frac{6}{10}$

11 $\frac{4}{5}$ ◯ $\frac{4}{10}$

12 $\frac{3}{4}$ ◯ $\frac{3}{10}$

☆ **Tell how you compare fractions.**

●●◯

Name _____

Write a number to make each comparison true.

1 $\dfrac{3}{4}$ > $\dfrac{\square}{4}$

2 $\dfrac{2}{2}$ = $\dfrac{3}{\square}$

3 $\dfrac{1}{8}$ < $\dfrac{\square}{8}$

4 $\dfrac{4}{5}$ > $\dfrac{\square}{5}$

5 $\dfrac{2}{4}$ > $\dfrac{\square}{4}$

6 $\dfrac{2}{2}$ = $\dfrac{2}{\square}$

7 $\dfrac{3}{6}$ < $\dfrac{\square}{6}$

8 $\dfrac{1}{3}$ > $\dfrac{1}{\square}$

9 $\dfrac{1}{2}$ > $\dfrac{\square}{\square}$

10 $\dfrac{1}{8}$ < $\dfrac{\square}{\square}$

11 $\dfrac{3}{5}$ > $\dfrac{\square}{\square}$

12 $\dfrac{2}{4}$ $\square$ $\dfrac{2}{6}$

13 $\dfrac{1}{3}$ > $\dfrac{\square}{\square}$

14 $\dfrac{1}{8}$ < $\dfrac{\square}{\square}$

15 $\dfrac{2}{4}$ < $\dfrac{\square}{\square}$

 How do you know that $\dfrac{1}{2}$ is greater than $\dfrac{1}{8}$?

Name _____

Write a number to make each comparison true.

1 A pizza has 8 slices. 3 slices have mushroom. 5 slices have pepperoni. Does the pizza have a greater portion of mushroom or pepperoni slices?

$$\frac{3}{8} \bigcirc \frac{\square}{\square}$$

2 Jamie and Ally both have the same amount of grapes. Jamie ate two-thirds of his grapes. Ally ate two-sixths of her grapes. Who ate a greater amount of grapes?

3 Maya buys 8 bananas. She eats one-fourth of the bananas on Monday. She eats one-eighth of the bananas on Wednesday. On which day does Maya eat fewer bananas?

4 Jake has 6 cards. 4 of his cards are red and 2 cards are blue. Alicia also has 6 cards. Half of her cards are red. Who has more red cards?

5 Miranda has read one-half of a chapter in her book. Miranda's chapter is 6 pages long. Which equation shows the number of pages Miranda has read?

a) $\frac{1}{2} = \frac{3}{6}$

b) $\frac{1}{2} = \frac{6}{6}$

c) $\frac{1}{2} = \frac{6}{6}$

d) $\frac{1}{2} = \frac{6}{6}$

6 Amelia has finished two-fourths of her math homework. Ben has 3 pages of math homework. He has finished 2 pages. Who has finished more of their homework? Circle the answer that best represents this problem.

a) $\frac{1}{2} = \frac{2}{4}$

b) $\frac{2}{4} > \frac{2}{3}$

c) $\frac{2}{4} < \frac{2}{3}$

d) $\frac{2}{4} > \frac{1}{3}$

Unit 18
Time to the Minute

Standard

Measurement & Data

Solve problems involving measurement and estimation of intervals of time, liquid volumes, and masses of objects.

3.MD.1. Tell and write time to the nearest minute and measure time intervals in minutes. Solve word problems involving addition and subtraction of time intervals in minutes, e.g., by representing the problem on a number line diagram.

Model the Skill

◆ Display a demonstration analog clock. Review the parts of the clock. Have students identify the hour hand, the minute hand, and the numbers on the clock face.

◆ **Ask:** *How can we use a clock to tell time?* (Possible response: look at the numbers that the hour hand and minute hand point to) **Say:** *The hour hand tells what hour it is. The minute hand tells how many minutes before or after the hour it is. There are 60 minutes in an hour. Each mark on the clock shows one minute. The marks on the clock can help us tell time to the minute.*

◆ Draw a clock that shows 10:15. **Ask:** *What number does the hour hand point to?* (10) *What number does the minute hand point to?* (15) *What time does the clock show?* (10:15) Demonstrate how to record the time. Remind students that the colon separates the hours from the minutes.

◆ Assign students the appropriate practice page(s) to support their understanding of the skill.

Assess the Skill

Use the following problems to pre-/post-assess students' understanding of the skill.

Name _____

Write the time two ways. Write the missing numbers.

1

____ : ____

20 minutes after ____

2

____ : ____

____ minutes after 10

3

____ : ____

____ minutes after 8

4

____ : ____

half past ____

5

____ : ____

half past ____

6

____ : ____

____ minutes after 11

 Draw a new minute hand on clocks 5 and 6 that shows 10 minutes later.

●○○

Name _____

Write the time two ways. Write the missing numbers.

1

____ : ____

____ minutes after 7

2

____ : ____

____ minutes after ____

3

____ : ____

13 minutes before ____

4

____ : ____

____ minutes before ____

10 minutes later ____ : ____

5

____ : ____

____ minutes after ____

10 minutes later ____ : ____

6

____ : ____

____ minutes before ____

10 minutes later ____ : ____

☆ **Tell where the minute hand is pointing on clocks 5 and 6.**

Name _____

Write the time. Then write the time 10 minutes later.

1 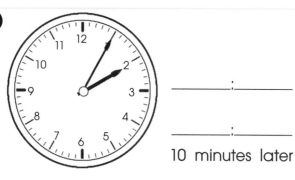 _____:_____

_____:_____
10 minutes later

2  _____:_____

_____:_____
10 minutes later

3  _____:_____

_____:_____
10 minutes later

4  _____:_____

_____:_____
10 minutes later

5  _____:_____

_____:_____
10 minutes later

6  _____:_____

_____:_____
10 minutes later

7  _____:_____

_____:_____
10 minutes later

8    _____:_____

_____:_____
10 minutes later

☆ **Tell where the clock hands point when it is 10 minutes later.**

Write how many minutes have passed.

  Start at 4:00 A.M.
End at 4:22 A.M.
_____ minutes have passed.

 Start at 8:30 A.M.
End at 8:45 A.M.
_____ minutes have passed.

  Start at 10:40 P.M.
End at 10:56 P.M.
_____ minutes have passed.

 Start at 2:58 A.M.
End at 3:07 A.M.
_____ minutes have passed.

  Start at 8:10 A.M.
End at 8:42 A.M.
_____ minutes have passed.

 Start at 11:50 A.M.
End at 12:02 P.M.
_____ minutes have passed.

  Start at 9:31 P.M.
End at 9:49 P.M.
_____ minutes have passed.

 Start at 1:07 A.M.
End at 2:00 A.M.
_____ minutes have passed.

Unit 19
Grams, Kilograms, Liters

Standard

Measurement & Data

Solve problems involving measurement and estimation of intervals of time, liquid volumes, and masses of objects.

3.MD.2. Measure and estimate liquid volumes and masses of objects using standard units of grams (g), kilograms (kg), and liters (l). Add, subtract, multiply, or divide to solve one-step word problems involving masses or volumes that are given in the same units, e.g., by using drawings (such as a beaker with a measurement scale) to represent the problem.

Model the Skill

Hand out identical objects, such as pencils or nickel coins to each student.

◆ **Say:** *Today we are going to learn about mass. The mass of an object tells the amount of matter in that object. On Earth, it also tells us how heavy an object is. You can measure mass in grams or kilograms. One kilogram is equal in mass to 1,000 grams.* Display a balance and some gram weights. **Say:** *I could use grams and a balance to measure the mass of a crayon or an eraser. What other objects might I measure this way?* (Possible response: small, light objects such as paper or a pen) Allow students to brainstorm other objects that might be measured using grams and a balance, and other objects that might be measured using kilograms and a scale.

◆ Have students work together to estimate and then measure their nickels. To help students estimate, have them hold the weights and the object they will measure. Remind students that an estimate is a thoughtful guess.

◆ **Ask:** *Would it be better to use grams or kilograms to measure the mass of a cat? Why?* (Possible response: kilograms because grams are too small a unit of measurement) Have students suggest other items that might be measured better in grams or kilograms.

◆ Assign students the appropriate practice page(s) to support their understanding of the skill.

Assess the Skill

Use the following problems to pre-/post-assess students' understanding of the skill.

◆ **Say:** *Estimate and then find the mass of the following objects:*
  • *a ruler*
  • *a pen*
  • *a shoe*
  • *a full bookbag or backpack*

Name _____

Circle your estimate for the mass of each object. Then measure. Complete the chart.

❶ Mass of Objects

Object	Estimate	Measure
pencil	5 grams 5 kilograms	
stack of books	5 grams 5 kilograms	

Circle your estimate for the capacity of each object. Then measure. Complete the chart.

❷ Capacity of Objects

Object	Estimate	Measure
paper cup	less than 1 liter more than 1 liter	
large bottle of milk	less than 1 liter more than 1 liter	

 Draw something that has a mass of about 1 kilogram.

Name _____

Circle the better estimate of the mass of each item pictured.

❶
bananas
1 gram
1 kilogram

❷
paper clip
1 gram
1 kilogram

❸
dog
10 grams
10 kilograms

❹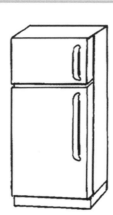
refrigerator
200 grams
200 kilograms

Circle the better estimate of the capacity of each item pictured.

❺
water bottle
1 liter
10 liters

❻
bird bath
1 liter
5 liters

❼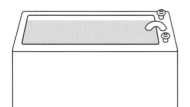
bath tub
5 liters
50 liters

❽
saucepan
3 liters
30 liters

☆ **Measure the mass of Item 2. Tell how you know your answer is reasonable.**

Name _____

Estimate the mass and capacity of each container. Then measure.

1 **Mass**

Object	Estimate	Measure
paper cup		
large bottle		
teaspoon		

2 **Capacity**

Object	Estimate More or less than a liter?	Measure More or less than a liter?
paper cup		
large bottle		
teaspoon		

☆ **Tell something that has a capacity of about 1 liter.**

How much will each container hold? Circle the better estimate.

  **drinking glass**
more than a liter
less than a liter

  **soup can**
more than a liter
less than a liter

  **pitcher**
3 liters
30 liters

  **fish tank**
2 liters
20 liters

Circle the correct answer for each question.

5 Olivia has a bath tub full of water. About how much water is in the bath tub?

a) 40 grams

b) 4 kilograms

c) 4 liters

d) 40 liters

6 Rex has toaster in his kitchen. What is the approximate mass of his toaster?

a) 10 grams

b) 1 kilogram

c) 1 liter

d) 10 liters

Unit 20
Measure Length to the Nearest Quarter Inch

Standard

Measurement & Data

Represent and interpret data.

3.MD.4. Generate measurement data by measuring lengths using rulers marked with halves and fourths of an inch. Show the data by making a line plot, where the horizontal scale is marked off in appropriate units—whole numbers, halves, or quarters.

Model the Skill

Hand out rulers and unsharpened pencils.

◆ **Say:** *You can use an inch ruler to measure the length of an object.* Have students look at the ruler. Help them identify the $\frac{1}{4}$-inch and $\frac{1}{2}$-inch marks on the ruler. Point out that the $\frac{1}{2}$-inch mark is the same as $\frac{2}{4}$. Have students identify specific points on the ruler, such as $1\frac{1}{2}$ inches, $2\frac{1}{4}$ inches, and $4\frac{3}{4}$ inches.

◆ **Ask:** *What is the length of the unsharpened pencil to the nearest half inch?* ($7\frac{1}{2}$ inches) *How did you find your answer?* (Possible response: I looked for the number on the ruler that is closest to the end of the pencil.) *We can say the length of the ruler is $7\frac{1}{2}$ inches to the nearest half inch.*

◆ Assign students the appropriate practice page(s) to support their understanding of the skill.

Assess the Skill

Use the following problems to pre-/post-assess students' understanding of the skill.

◆ **Say:** *Estimate and then find the length of the following objects:*
• *a book*
• *a desk*
• *a tissue box*
• *a calculator*

Name _____

Measure the length of each string to the nearest quarter inch.

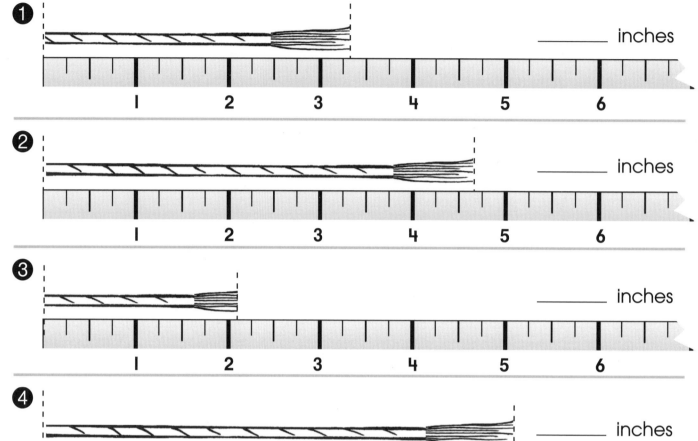

❶ _____ inches

❷ _____ inches

❸ _____ inches

❹ _____ inches

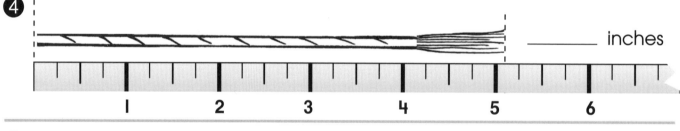

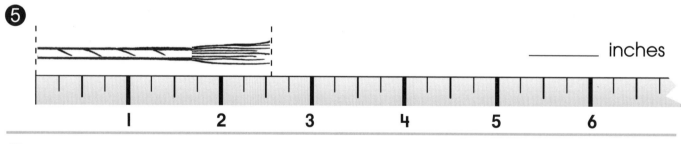

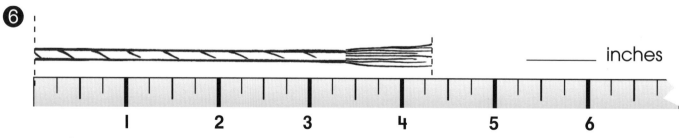

❺ _____ inches

❻ _____ inches

☆ **Circle the longest piece of string.**

●○○

Use an inch ruler. Measure each pencil to the nearest quarter inch.

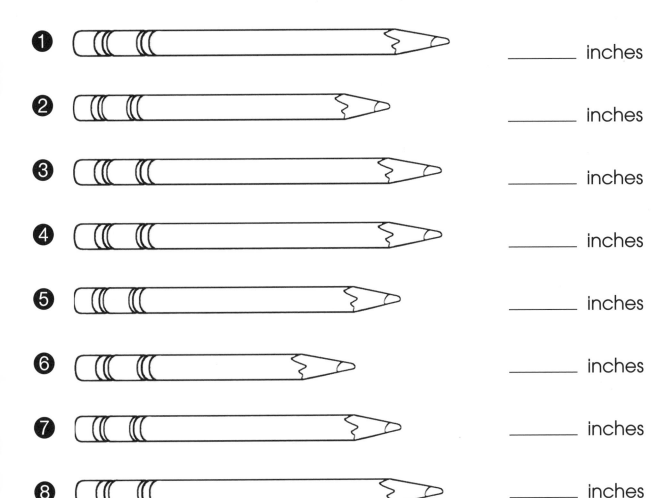

❶ _____ inches

❷ _____ inches

❸ _____ inches

❹ _____ inches

❺ _____ inches

❻ _____ inches

❼ _____ inches

❽ _____ inches

Use the data to make a line plot.

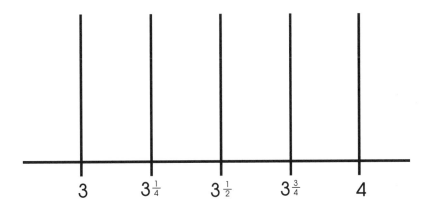

Length of Pencils in Inches

 Tell how you measured.

Name _____

Use an inch ruler. Measure the length of 10 crayons. Measure to the nearest quarter inch. Record the data. Use the data to make a line plot. Make an X to show the length of each crayon.

Crayon #	Crayon Length
1	
2	
3	
4	
5	
6	
7	
8	
9	
10	

Length of Crayons in Inches	Number of Crayons

☆ **Write an explanation of how the data in the chart matches the line plot.**

Name _____

Solve.

1 Sam measured the lengths of his crayons. The table shows his data. Use Sam's data to complete the line plot. Make an X to show the length of each crayon.

Length of Crayons in Inches	Number of Crayons
3	|
$3\frac{1}{4}$	|||
$3\frac{1}{2}$	⊬⊬
$3\frac{3}{4}$	|
4	

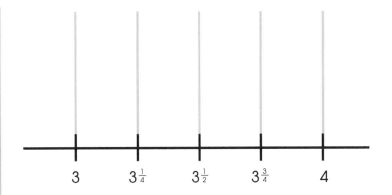

Length of Crayons in Inches

2 What length was the most common of Sam's crayons?

a) 4

b) $3\frac{3}{4}$

c) $3\frac{1}{2}$

d) $3\frac{1}{4}$

3 How many crayons were more than 3 inches in length?

a) 3

b) 4

c) 7

d) 9

Unit 21
Make and Use Pictographs

Standard

Measurement & Data

Represent and interpret data.

3.MD.3. Draw a scaled picture graph and a scaled bar graph to represent a data set with several categories. Solve one- and two-step "how many more" and "how many less" problems using information presented in scaled bar graphs. For example, draw a bar graph in which each square in the bar graph might represent 5 pets.

Model the Skill

Draw the following pictograph on the board.

Favorite Juices

Each ▽ stands for 2 votes.

◆ **Say:** *Today we are going to learn about pictographs. Pictographs are graphs that use pictures or symbols to show information or data. What is the title of the graph?* (Favorite Juices) *What are the juice choices?* (apple, grape, and orange) *What does each cup stand for?* (2 votes) *How do you know?* (Possible response: The key under the graph tells you.)

◆ **Ask:** *Which juice got the most votes? How do you know?* (grape; possible explanation: it has the most cups/votes) Have students share their strategies.

◆ **Ask:** *How many students voted for orange juice?* (3) *How can you tell by looking at the graph?* (Possible response: I see there is a half cup, which would mean half of 2, which is 1.)

◆ **Ask:** *How many more students voted for grape juice than apple juice?* (2) Have students discuss other strategies such as subtracting the number of votes for apple juice from the number of votes for grape juice.

◆ Assign students the appropriate practice page(s) to support their understanding of the skill.

Assess the Skill

Use the following problem to pre-/post-assess students' understanding of the skill.

◆ **Say:** *Interview your classmates. Ask them to vote on their favorite sandwich or favorite fruit. Then share the data in a pictograph.*

Name _____

Use the pictograph to answer each question.

Mr. Smith's class made a pictograph.
The graph shows the students' favorite juices.

Favorite Juices

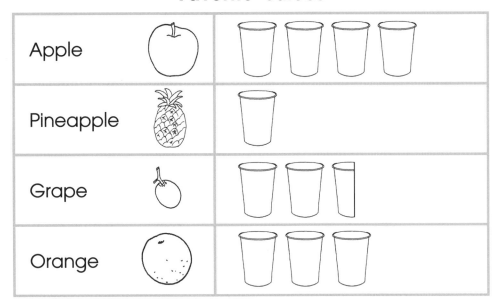

Each ▽ **stands for 2 votes.**

1 Which juice got the most votes? _____

2 How many more students voted for apple juice than orange juice?
_____ more students

3 How many students voted for grape juice? _____ students

4 How many fewer students voted for pineapple juice than
apple juice? _____ fewer students

☆ **Circle the juice flavor that received an odd number of votes.**

Name _____

Complete each pictograph. Then answer the questions.

1 Lea sold 14 tickets to the class play. Kim sold 8 tickets. Tom sold 12 tickets.

5 Addy sold 5 apples at the fair. Casey sold 10 apples. Finn sold 12 apples.

Tickets Sold

Each [ADMIT ONE] stands for 4 tickets.

Apples Sold

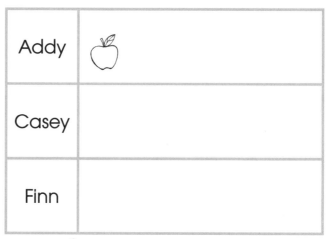

Each 🍎 stands for 2 apples.

Use the graph to answer each question.

2 How many more tickets did Lea sell than Tom?

_____ more tickets

3 How many fewer tickets did Kim sell than Tom?

_____ fewer tickets

4 How many fewer tickets did Kim sell than Lea?

_____ fewer tickets

Use the graph to answer each question.

6 How many more apples did Finn sell than Casey?

_____ more apples

7 How many fewer apples did Addy sell than Finn?

_____ fewer apples

8 How many fewer apples did Addy sell than Casey?

_____ fewer apples

 Tell how you completed each pictograph.

●●●○

Name _____

Complete each pictograph. Then answer the questions.

1 Gina took a poll of favorite lunch in her class. Grilled cheese got 6 votes. Veggie burritos got 3 votes. Hamburgers got 4 votes and pizza got 11 votes.

Favorite Lunches

Each ☺ stands for _____ votes.

Use the graph to answer each question.

2 How many more votes did pizza get than hamburgers?

_____

3 How many more votes did grilled cheese get than hamburgers?

_____

4 How many fewer votes did veggie burritos get than pizza?

_____

5 Chris took a poll of favorite sports in his class. Soccer got 9 votes. Baseball got 12 votes. Football got 6 votes and basketball got 6 votes.

Favorite Sports

Each ☺ stands for _____ votes.

Use the graph to answer each question.

6 How many more votes did baseball get than soccer?

_____

7 How many fewer votes did football get than baseball?

_____

8 How many fewer votes did basketball get than football?

_____

 Explain how you made your key.

Name _____

Complete each pictograph. Then answer the questions.

1 Renee sold 30 tickets to the school raffle. Bobby sold 40 tickets. Lizzy sold 35 tickets.

5 Max got 8 votes for class president. Riley got 10 votes. Alisa got 7 votes.

Tickets Sold

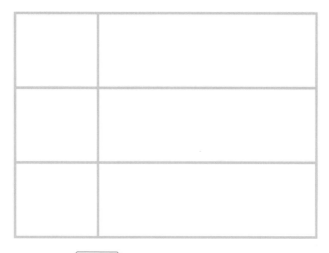

= _____ tickets

Votes for Class President

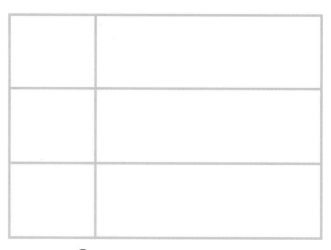

☺ = _____ votes

Use the graph to answer each question.

2 How many more tickets did Lizzy sell than Renee?

_____ more tickets

3 How many fewer tickets did Renee sell than Bobby?

_____ fewer tickets

4 How many fewer tickets did Lizzy sell than Bobby?

_____ fewer tickets

Use the graph to answer each question.

6 How many more votes did Max get than Alisa?

_____ more votes

7 How many fewer votes did Alisa get than Riley?

_____ fewer votes

8 How many fewer votes did Max get than Riley?

_____ fewer votes

Unit 22
Make and Use Bar Graphs

Standard

Measurement & Data

Represent and interpret data.

3.MD.3. Draw a scaled picture graph and a scaled bar graph to represent a data set with several categories. Solve one- and two-step "how many more" and "how many less" problems using information presented in scaled bar graphs. For example, draw a bar graph in which each square in the bar graph might represent 5 pets.

Model the Skill

Copy the following bar graph onto the board.

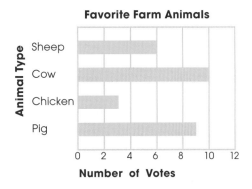

◆ **Say:** *Today we are going to learn about bar graphs. Bar graphs are graphs that use bars to show information or data. What is the title of this graph?* (Favorite Farm Animals) *What are the animal types?* (sheep, cow, chicken, pig) *What does each axis show?* (The x axis, or horizontal axis, shows the number of votes and the y-axis, or the vertical axis, shows the type of animal.) *How do you know?* (Possible response: because each axis is labeled)

◆ **Ask:** *Which animal got the most votes? How do you know?* (cow; possible explanation: that bar is the longest) Have students share their strategies.

◆ **Ask:** *How many more students voted for pig than chicken?* (6) *How can you tell by looking at the graph?* Have students discuss other strategies such as subtracting the number of votes for chicken from the number of votes for pig.

◆ Assign students the appropriate practice page(s) to support their understanding of the skill.

Assess the Skill

Use the following activity to pre-/post-assess students' understanding of the skill.

◆ **Say:** *Interview your classmates. Ask them to vote on their favorite type of pet or favorite sandwich. Then share the data in a bar graph.*

Name _____

Use the bar graph to answer each question.

The students in Ms. Pier's class voted for their favorite farm animal. The bar graph shows the results.

Use the bar graph to answer each question.

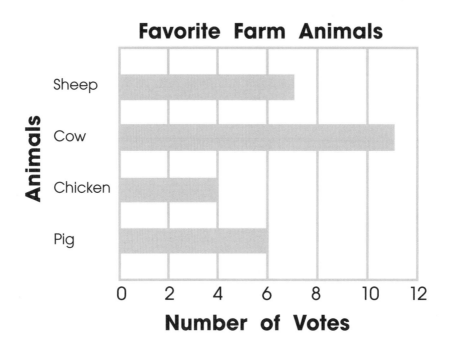

Favorite Farm Animals

❶ How many more students voted for sheep than pig?
_____ more students

❷ How many fewer students voted for pig than cow?
_____ fewer students

❸ How many more students voted for cow than chicken?
_____ more students

❹ How many fewer students voted for chicken than sheep?
_____ fewer students

☆ Circle the two farm animals that got the most votes.

Complete each bar graph. Then answer each question.

The students in the fourth grade voted for their favorite pet. Cat received 9 votes, dog got 14 votes, hamster got 6 votes, and fish got 10 votes.

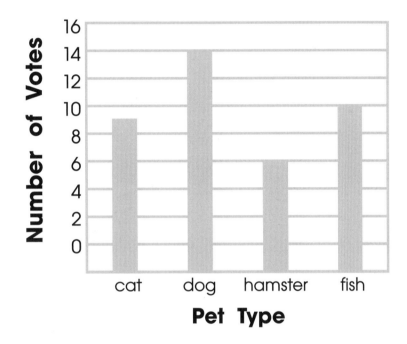

1 How many more students voted for cat than hamster?
_____ more students

2 How many fewer students voted for fish than dog?
_____ fewer students

3 How many more students voted for fish than cat?
_____ more students

4 How many fewer students voted for hamster than dog?
_____ fewer students

 Tell how you found your answers.

Name _____

Complete each bar graph. Then answer each question.

❶ Rachel sold 18 muffins at the bake sale. Perry sold 20 muffins. Kayam sold 25 muffins.

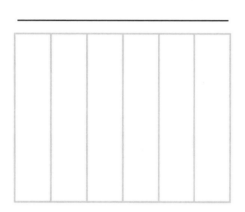

Name of Student

Number of Muffins

Use your graph to answer each question.

❷ How many more muffins did Perry sell than Rachel?

_____ more muffins

❸ How many fewer muffins did Perry sell than Kayam?

_____ fewer muffins

❹ How many fewer muffins did Rachel sell than Kayam?

_____ fewer muffins

❺ Buster read 40 pages over the weekend. Phoebe read 60 pages. William read 55 pages.

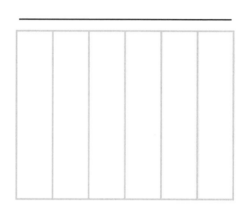

Name of Student

Number of Pages

Use your graph to answer each question.

❻ How many more pages did Phoebe read than William?

_____ more pages

❼ How many fewer pages did Phoebe read than Buster and William combined?

_____ fewer pages

❽ How many pages did they read in all?

_____ pages

☆ **Write a description of how you completed the labels for each axis.**

Complete each bar graph. Then answer each question.

1 Fred took a poll of favorite sandwiches in his class. Bologna got 10 votes. Tuna got 8 votes. Turkey got 7 votes and ham got 9 votes.

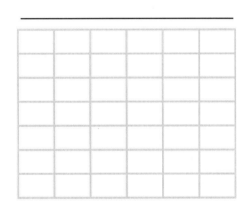

Number of Votes

_____

Type of Sandwich

5 The school store sold many items on Monday. The store sold 200 pairs of scissors, 400 notebooks, 500 pens, and 550 pencils.

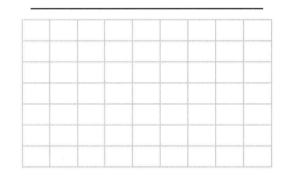

Number of Items

_____

Items

Use your bar graph to answer each question.

2 What two sandwiches are the most popular?

_____ _____

3 How many more votes did bologna get than turkey?
_____ more votes

4 How many fewer votes did turkey get than ham?
_____ fewer votes

Use your bar graph to answer each question.

6 How many more pencils were sold than pens?
_____ more pencils

7 How many fewer scissors were sold than notebooks?
_____ fewer scissors

8 How many fewer scissors were sold than pencils?
_____ fewer scissors

Unit 23
Understand Perimeter

Standard

Measurement & Data

Geometric measurement: recognize perimeter as an attribute of plane figures and distinguish between linear and area measures.

3.MD.8. Solve real world and mathematical problems involving perimeters of polygons, including finding the perimeter given the side lengths, finding an unknown side length, and exhibiting rectangles with the same perimeter and different areas or with the same area and different perimeters.

Model the Skill

Draw the following figures on the board.

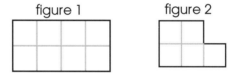

figure 1   figure 2

◆ **Say:** *Today we are going to learn about perimeter. Perimeter is the distance around a figure.* Have students look at figure 1. Demonstrate how to find the length of each side.

◆ **Ask:** *What shape is this figure?* (rectangle) *What is the perimeter? How do you know?* (12 units; possible explanation: there are 12 units around the rectangle, so the perimeter is 12; add the length of each side)

◆ Have students look at figure 2. **Ask:** *How is this figure different from figure 1?* (Possible response: This is not a rectangle; this figure looks like a square with an extra square unit.) Point out that students can still tell the perimeter of the figure by counting the number of units. Help students find the length of each side.

◆ Assign students the appropriate practice page(s) to support their understanding of the skill.

Assess the Skill

Use the following problems to pre-/post-assess students' understanding of the skill.

◆ **Say:** *Find the perimeter of a book, your desk, a piece of paper. Draw a closed shape with a perimeter of 18 inches.*

Find the perimeter. Count the units.

❶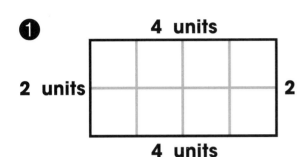

4 units

2 units   **2 units**

4 units

❷

2 units

2 units

1 unit

1 unit

Perimeter: _____ units   Perimeter: _____ units

❸ 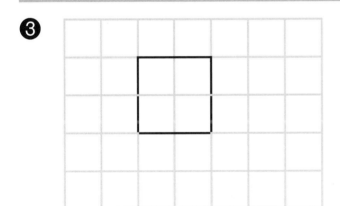   ❹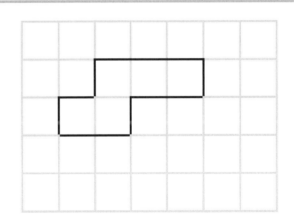

Perimeter: _____ units   Perimeter: _____ units

 Tell how you counted the units to find the perimeter.

Name _____

Draw a closed figure. Write the perimeter.

❶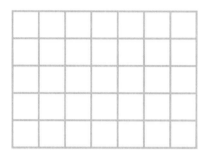

Perimeter: _____ units

❷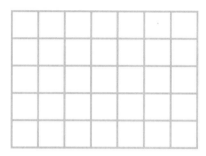

Perimeter: _____ units

Draw a closed figure to match the perimeter.

❸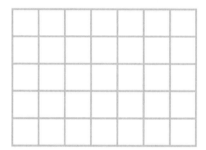

Perimeter: 8 units

❹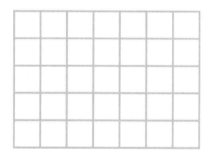

Perimeter: 10 units

❺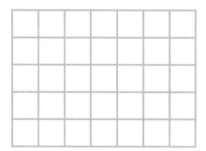

Perimeter: 9 units

❻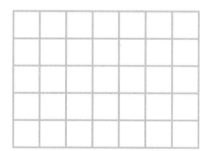

Perimeter: 16 units

 Tell how you found the perimeter.

Name _____

Add to find the perimeter.

1

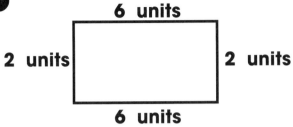

6 units

2 units   2 units

6 units

Perimeter: _____ units

2

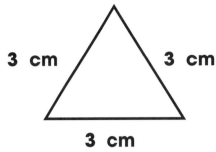

3 cm   3 cm

3 cm

3 + 3 + 3 = _____

Perimeter: _____ centimeters

3

4 cm

3 cm   2 cm

5 cm

Perimeter: _____ centimeters

4

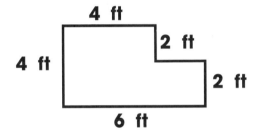

4 ft

2 ft

4 ft

2 ft

6 ft

Perimeter: _____ feet

5

3 cm   5 cm

4 cm

Perimeter: _____ centimeters

6

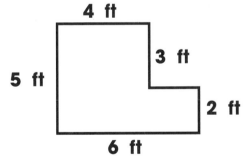

4 ft

3 ft

5 ft

2 ft

6 ft

Perimeter: _____ feet

 Tell how you found the perimeter.

Name _____

Solve.

1 A rectangle has a length of 8 units and a width of 3 units. What is the perimeter of the rectangle?

2 A square has a length of 16 units. What is the perimeter of the square?

3 The garden is a rectangle with a length of 20 feet and a width of 15 feet. What is the perimeter of the garden?

4 The rectangular floor has a length of 14 meters and a width of 11 meters. What is the perimeter of the room?

5 Ashley has a picture that is 11 inches tall and 8 inches wide. How much wood trim does she need to frame the perimeter of the picture?

a) 27 inches

b) 38 inches

c) 40 inches

d) 88 inches

6 The figure below is a diagram of John's yard. If John buys fence to run along the perimeter of his yard, how much fence will he need?

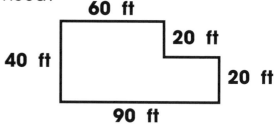

a) 210 feet

b) 230 feet

c) 240 feet

d) 260 feet

Unit 24
Understand Area

Standard

Measurement & Data

Geometric measurement: understand concepts of area and relate area to multiplication and to addition.

3.MD.5. Recognize area as an attribute of plane figures and understand concepts of area measurement.

3.MD.6. Measure areas by counting unit squares (square cm, square m, square in, square ft, and improvised units).

3.MD.7. Relate area to the operations of multiplication and addition.

Geometric measurement: recognize perimeter as an attribute of plane figures and distinguish between linear and area measures.

3.MD.8. Solve real world and mathematical problems involving perimeters of polygons, including finding the perimeter given the side lengths, finding an unknown side length, and exhibiting rectangles with the same perimeter and different areas or with the same area and different perimeters.

Model the Skill

Draw the following figures on the board.

figure 1   figure 2

◆ **Say:** *Today we are going to learn about area. Area is the number of square units that are needed to cover a flat surface.* Have students look at figure 1 and identify one square unit. **Ask:** *What figure do the square units make?* (rectangle) *You can count the square units in the rectangle to find its area. How many square units are in the rectangle?* (8) *We can say that the area of this rectangle is 8 square units.*

◆ Have students look at figure 2. **Ask:** *How is this figure different from figure 1?* (Possible response: This is not a rectangle; this figure has more sides, fewer square units.) Point out that students can still tell the area of the figure by counting the number of square units. (5) Allow students to use square tiles if they wish to model the figure, and then find the area.

◆ Assign students the appropriate practice page(s) to support their understanding of the skill.

Assess the Skill

Use the following problems to pre-/post-assess students' understanding of the skill.

◆ **Say:** *Find the area of a tabletop, desktop, or a piece of paper. Draw a closed shape with an area of 18 inches.*

Name _____

Count the square units to find the area.

❶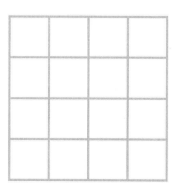

_____ square units

❷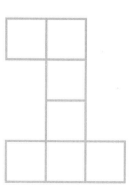

_____ square units

❸

_____ square units

❹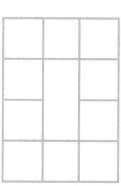

_____ square units

❺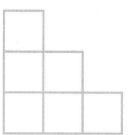

_____ square units

❻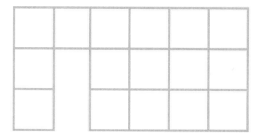

_____ square units

☆ **Tell how you got your answers.**

Unit 24 • Common Core Mathematics Grade 3 • ©2012 Newmark Learning, LLC

Draw a figure to match the area.

1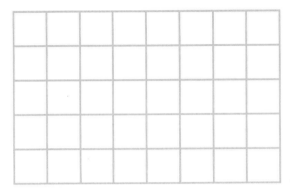

4 square units

2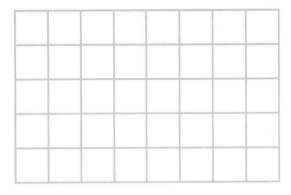

9 square units

3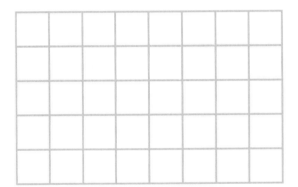

8 square units

4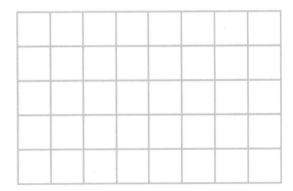

12 square units

5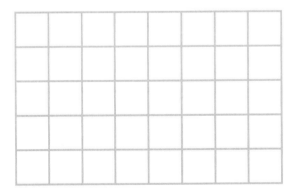

14 square units

6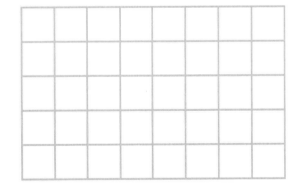

18 square units

☆ **Tell how you know your figure shows an area of 12 square units.**

Name _____

Add to find the area.

 1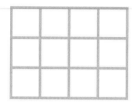

4 squares in each row, 3 rows

4 + 4 + 4 = _____

Area: _____ square units

2

___ squares in each row, ___ rows

5 + 5 = _____

Area: _____ square units

3

_____

Area: _____ square units

4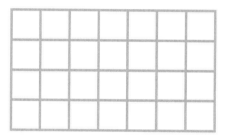

_____

Area: _____ square units

5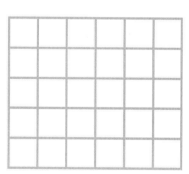

_____

Area: _____ square units

6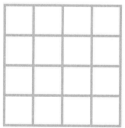

_____

Area: _____ square units

 Tell another addition sentence you can use to find the area.

●●●

Name _____

Solve.

1 A rectangle has a length of 6 units and a width of 4 units. What is the area of the rectangle?

2 A square has a length of 5 units. What is the area of the square?

3 The rug is a rectangle with a length of 10 feet and a width of 8 feet. What is the area of the garden?

4 The tabletop has a length of 5 meters and a width of 2 meters. What is the area of the table?

5 The gym floor has a length of 30 yards and a width of 20 yards. What is the area of the gym?

a) 100 yards

b) 100 square yards

c) 600 yards

d) 600 square yards

6 Esther's patio is 9 feet long and 7 feet wide. If Esther covers the patio in 1 square-foot tiles, how many tiles will she need?

a) 16 tiles

b) 32 tiles

c) 63 tiles

d) 126 tiles

Unit 25
Find Area

Standard

Measurement & Data

Geometric measurement: understand concepts of area and relate area to multiplication and to addition.

3.MD.5. Recognize area as an attribute of plane figures and understand concepts of area measurement.

3.MD.6. Measure areas by counting unit squares (square cm, square m, square in, square ft, and improvised units).

3.MD.7. Relate area to the operations of multiplication and addition.

Geometric measurement: recognize perimeter as an attribute of plane figures and distinguish between linear and area measures.

3.MD.8. Solve real world and mathematical problems involving perimeters of polygons, including finding the perimeter given the side lengths, finding an unknown side length, and exhibiting rectangles with the same perimeter and different areas or with the same area and different perimeters.

Model the Skill

Draw the following rectangle on the board.

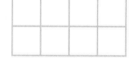

◆ **Say:** *Today we are going to learn about the different ways to find area. Area is the number of square units that are needed to cover a flat surface.* Have students look at the rectangle and identify one square unit. **Ask:** *How can you find the area of this rectangle?* (count square units, add rows or columns) *You can also multiply the number of rows by the number of columns to find the area of a rectangle. You can multiply the length by the width.*

$$A = l \times w$$

◆ Help students count the length and width of the rectangle in units and then use the formula to find the area. **Ask:** *What is the area of the rectangle?* (8 square units)

◆ Assign students the appropriate practice page(s) to support their understanding of the skill. Allow students to use square tiles if they wish to model the figure, and then find the area.

Assess the Skill

Use the following problems to pre-/post-assess students' understanding of the skill.

◆ **Say:** *Find the area of a book, your desk, a piece of paper. Then draw a closed shape with an area of 16 square inches.*

Name _____

Count the square units to find the area.

1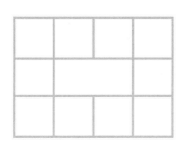

_____ square units

2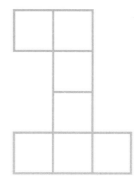

_____ square units

Add the square units to find the area.

3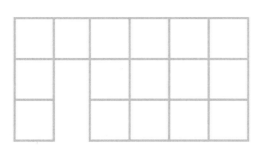

_____ square units

4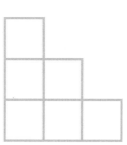

_____ square units

Multiply to find the area.

5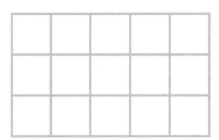

_____ square units

6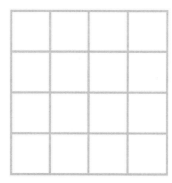

_____ square units

 Tell how you got your answer.

Name _____

Add to find the area.

 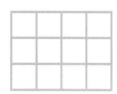

4 squares in each row, 3 rows

4 + 4 + 4 = _____

Area: _____ square units

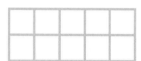

___ squares in each row, ___ rows

5 + 5 = _____

Area: _____ square units

Multiply to find the area. Use the formula $A = l \times w$.

length: _____ units

width: _____ units

Area:

_____ x _____ = _____ square units

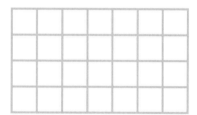

length: _____ units

width: _____ units

Area:

_____ x _____ = _____ square units

 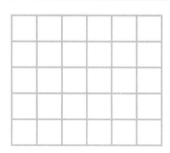

length: _____ units

width: _____ units

Area:

_____ x _____ = _____ square units

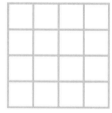

length: _____ units

width: _____ units

Area:

_____ x _____ = _____ square units

⭐ **Tell another addition sentence you can use to find the area.**

Name _____

Find the area.

❶

Count: _____ square units

Add:

4 + 4 = _____ square units

Multiply:

2 x 4 = _____ square units

❷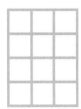

Count: _____ square units

Add:

3 + 3 + 3 + 3 = _____ square units

Multiply:

4 x 3 = _____ square units

Multiply to find the area. Use the formula $A = l$ **x** $w.$

❸

_____

_____

Area: _____ square units

❹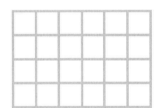

_____

_____

Area: _____ square units

❺

_____

_____

Area: _____ square units

❻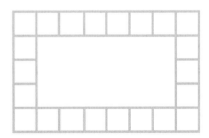

_____

_____

Area: _____ square units

☆ **Explain how you found the area in Problem 6.**

Name _____

Solve.

1 The floor is 6 meters in length and 4 meters in width. What is the area of the floor?

2 The garden is a rectangle. The width is 10 feet and the length is 15 feet. What is the area of the garden?

3 The baking pan is 9 inches wide and 20 inches long. If we cover the bottom of the pan with pastry dough, what is the area covered with dough?

4 Ruby's desktop is 30 centimeters wide and 20 centimeters long. What is the area of her desktop?

5 Stephen has a rectangular fence running along the perimeter of his yard. The length of the fence is 20 meters long. The yard area is 300 square meters. What is the width of the fence?

a) 15 square meters

b) 15 meters

c) 280 meters

d) 320 square meters

6 The area of the rectangular rug is 20 square feet. The width is 4 feet. What is the perimeter of the rug?

a) 24 feet

b) 24 square feet

c) 18 feet

d) 18 square feet

Unit 26
Quadrilaterals

Standard

Geometry

Reason with shapes and their attributes.

3.G.1. Understand that shapes in different categories (e.g., rhombuses, rectangles, and others) may share attributes (e.g., having four sides), and that the shared attributes can define a larger category (e.g., quadrilaterals). Recognize rhombuses, rectangles, and squares as examples of quadrilaterals, and draw examples of quadrilaterals that do not belong to any of these subcategories.

Model the Skill

Draw the following.

◆ **Say:** *We are going to learn about quadrilaterals today. A quadrilateral is a plane figure with four sides. A plane figure is a closed figure—it begins and ends at the same place.* Have students identify the open and closed figures.

◆ **Ask:** *What shape is figure 1?* (square) *How do you know the figure is a square?* (Possible response: It has four sides and four right angles.) *Is a square a quadrilateral? How do you know?* (Yes. It is a plane figure with four sides.)

◆ Have students look at the fifth figure. **Ask:** *What shape is this figure?* (open figure) *How many sides does this figure have? Is this figure a quadrilateral? Why or why not?* (No. It has 5 sides and it is not a closed figure.)

◆ Assign students the appropriate practice page(s) to support their understanding of the skill.

Assess the Skill

Use the following problems to pre-/post-assess students' understanding of the skill.

Have students draw a:

- square
- rectangle
- rhombus
- trapezoid

Name _____

Cross out the figure that does NOT belong.

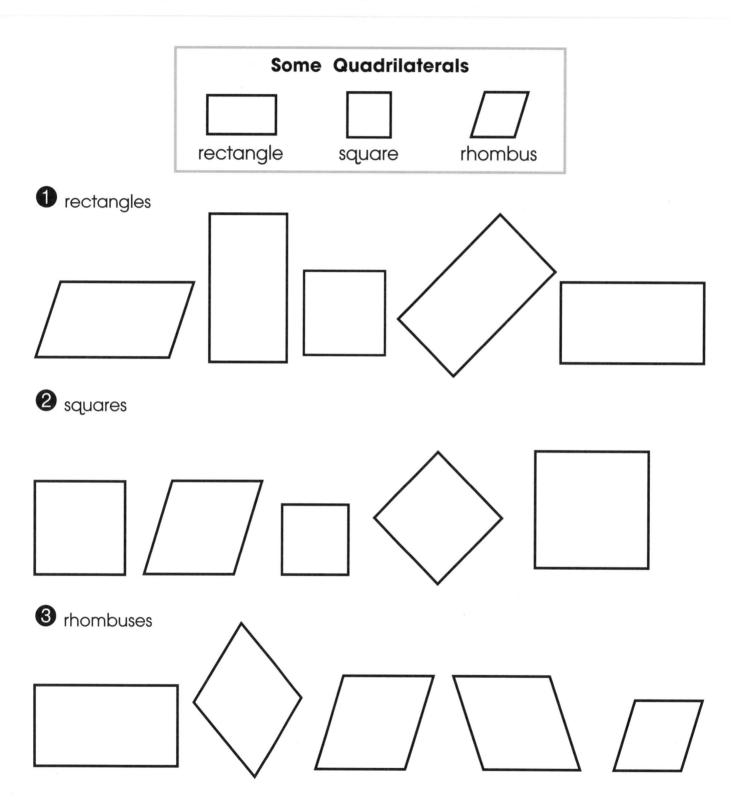

Some Quadrilaterals

rectangle   square   rhombus

❶ rectangles

❷ squares

❸ rhombuses

☆ **Tell how a rhombus and a square are different.**

Name _____

Draw a ring around each quadrilateral.

1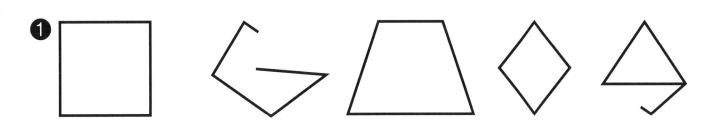

2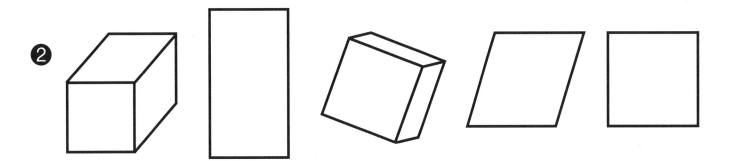

3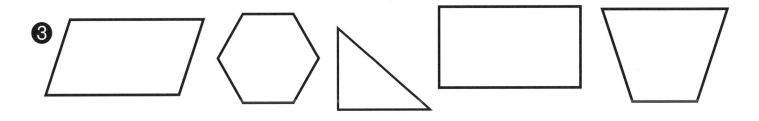

4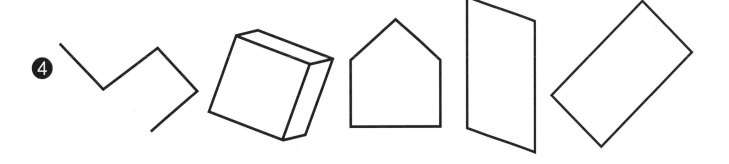

 Tell how you know which figure is a quadrilateral.

Name _____

Cross out the figures that do NOT belong.

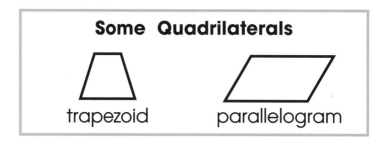

Some Quadrilaterals

trapezoid   parallelogram

❶ trapezoids

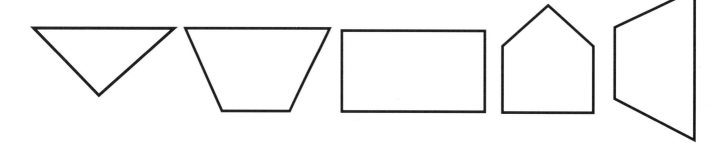

❷ squares

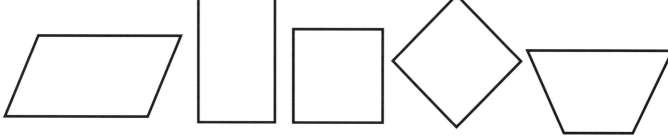

❸ rectangles

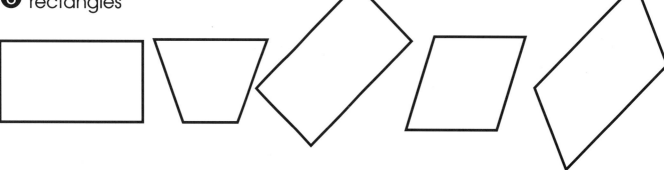

 Tell how a rectangle and a trapezoid are different.

Draw each figure.

 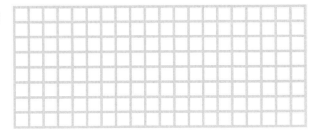

Draw a quadrilateral with
4 sides of equal lengths.

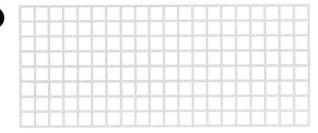

Draw a quadrilateral that is
NOT a rectangle.

 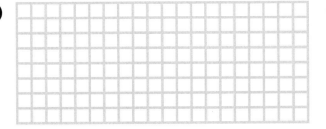

Draw a quadrilateral that does
NOT have 4 right angles.

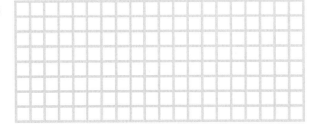

Draw a rhombus.

 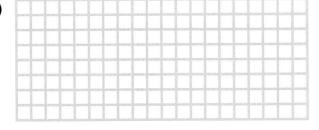

Draw a quadrilateral that is
NOT a square.

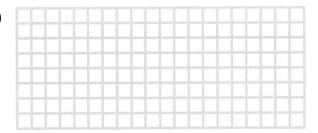

Draw a quadrilateral that has
2 sides of equal length and
no right angles.

Unit 27
Partition Shapes

Standard

Geometry

Reason with shapes and their attributes.

3.G.2. Partition shapes into parts with equal areas. Express the area of each part as a unit fraction of the whole. For example, partition a shape into 4 parts with equal area, and describe the area of each part as 1/4 of the area of the shape.

Model the Skill

◆ Hand out sheets of paper to each student.

◆ **Ask:** *What type of shape is this piece of paper?* (rectangle/quadrilateral) *Draw a line on this piece of paper so that the paper shows two equal shares. Each share of the paper is the same size. The shares are equal. How is this paper divided?* (into halves) *Each half of the rectangle is one-half.*

◆ **Say:** *Now draw another line on this piece of paper so that the paper shows four equal shares. What does the paper show now?* (fourths or quarters)

◆ Assign students the appropriate practice page(s) to support their understanding of the skill. If necessary, have students fold another sheet of paper to see the equal shares for halves, fourths, and thirds.

Assess the Skill

Use the following problems to pre-/post-assess students' understanding of the skill.

◆ **Ask:** *How would you partition each of these shapes into:*

• halves

• thirds

• fourths, or quarters

Name _____

Partition each shape as directed.

1 Show four equal shares.

2 Show two equal shares.

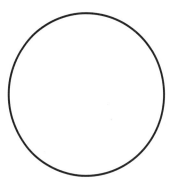

3 Show fourths.

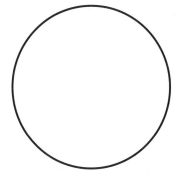

4 Show thirds.

Circle the shapes that show halves.

5

Circle the shapes that show fourths, or quarters.

6

☆ **Shade the shapes in Problems 1 and 3 to show one-fourth.**

Name _____

Shade one part of each shape. Then label what each shape shows.

❶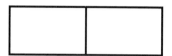

_____

❷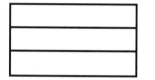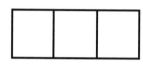

_____

❸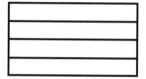

_____

❹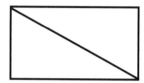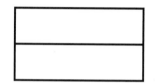

_____

Partition each shape. Then shade it to match its label.

❺ 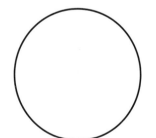 $\frac{1}{2}$

❻  $\frac{1}{4}$

❼ 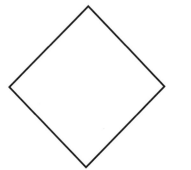 $\frac{2}{3}$

❽ 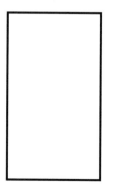 $\frac{2}{4}$

☆ **Tell how many ways you can partition a square into halves.**

●●○

Name _____

Partition each shape. Then shade it as directed.

1 one-half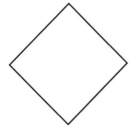

2 one-fourth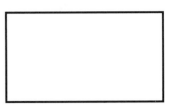

3 one-third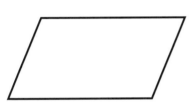

4 two-fourths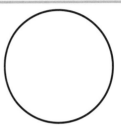

5 one-half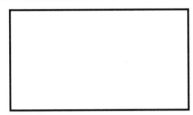

6 one-fourth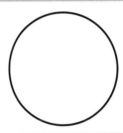

7 two-thirds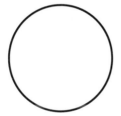

8 two-fourths

9 two-thirds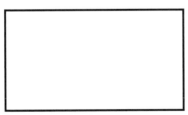

10 three-fourths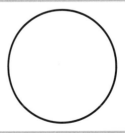

11 one-third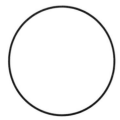

12 two-sixths

 Tell how many ways you can partition a rectangle into quarters.

Name _____

Find the area of each shape.

 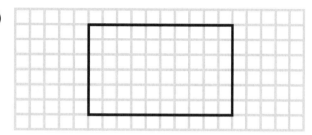

The area of the rectangle is 60 square units. What is the area of one-half of the rectangle?

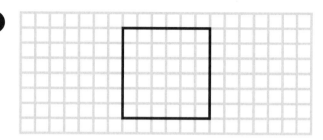

The area of the square is 36 square units. What is the area of one-fourth of the square?

 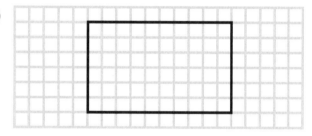

What is the area of one-third of this rectangle?

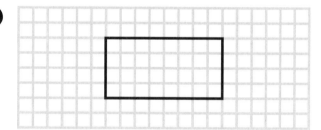

What is the area of two-fourths of this rectangle?

 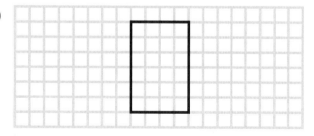

What is the area of two-halves of this rectangle?

What is the area of two-thirds of this rectangle?

Name _____

Round each number to complete the chart.

	Whole number	Rounded to the nearest ten	Rounded to the nearest hundred
1	562		
2	341		
3	282		
4	119		
5	706		
6	349		
7	461		
8	832		
9	925		
10		450	400
11	643		
12		550	

Name _____

Solve.

1   342
      − 17

2   129
      + 438

3   407
      − 23

4   688
      + 193

5 145 − 132

6 806 − 513

7 394 + 209

8 473 + 191

9 602 + 248

10 366 − 126

11 873 − 183

12 564 − 206

13 431 + 373

14 455 − 165

15 67 + 735

16 501 − 129

17 492 + 35

18 39 + 781

19 472 − 237

20 614 − 208

ommon Core Mathematics Grade 3 • ©2012 Newmark Learning, LLC

Name _____

Solve.

1   286
       − 72

2   204
       − 84

3   78
       + 463

4   205
       + 635

---

5   245 − 236

6   476 − 313

7   521 − 243

8   758 − 203

---

9   452 + 289

10 366 − 328

11 49 + 789

12 107 + 788

---

13 219 + 211

14 354 − 305

15 867 − 816

16 601 − 129

---

17 241 + 159

18 809 − 372

19 472 − 407

20 513 − 208

Name _____

Solve.

1 5 x 7

2 1 x 9

3 2 x 6

4 4 x 8

5 3 x 4

6 9 x 7

7 10 x 2

8 6 x 4

9 6 x 10

10 5 x 0

11 2 x 5

12 8 x 1

13 2 x 4

14 6 x 9

15 4 x 7

16 5 x 6

17 6 x 3

18 10 x 4

19 1 x 10

20 9 x 7

Common Core Mathematics Grade 3 • ©2012 Newmark Learning, LLC

Solve.

1 5 x 3   **2** 2 x 7   **3** 5 x 9   **4** 0 x 10

5 7 x 3   **6** 4 x 6   **7** 9 x 4   **8** 8 x 6

9 3 x 9   **10** 8 x 2   **11** 3 x 6   **12** 9 x 1

13 8 x 10   **14** 5 x 8   **15** 2 x 9   **16** 4 x 2

17 0 x 7   **18** 1 x 5   **19** 2 x 10   **20** 8 x 7

Name _____

Solve.

1   10 x 8   **2**   6 x 7   **3**   3 x 3   **4**   9 x 10

5   7 x 7   **6**   6 x 0   **7**   10 x 4   **8**   4 x 4

9   8 x 6   **10**   5 x 5   **11**   9 x 6   **12**   2 x 9

13   9 x 7   **14**   10 x 6   **15**   9 x 9   **16**   7 x 3

17   6 x 6   **18**   1 x 4   **19**   10 x 10   **20**   8 x 8

Common Core Mathematics Grade 3 • ©2012 Newmark Learning, LLC

Solve.

1 15 ÷ 5   **2** 9 ÷ 9   **3** 6 ÷ 6   **4** 8 ÷ 4

5 12 ÷ 4   **6** 49 ÷ 7   **7** 10 ÷ 2   **8** 12 ÷ 2

9 16 ÷ 8   **10** 5 ÷ 0   **11** 20 ÷ 5   **12** 8 ÷ 1

13 20 ÷ 4   **14** 63 ÷ 9   **15** 42 ÷ 7   **16** 54 ÷ 6

17 18 ÷ 3   **18** 16 ÷ 4   **19** 10 ÷ 10   **20** 21 ÷ 7

Name _____

Solve.

1 $8 \div 4$ **2** $18 \div 9$ **3** $20 \div 2$ **4** $15 \div 3$

5 $16 \div 2$ **6** $10 \div 5$ **7** $14 \div 2$ **8** $18 \div 3$

9 $24 \div 6$ **10** $9 \div 3$ **11** $21 \div 3$ **12** $8 \div 2$

13 $8 \div 4$ **14** $45 \div 5$ **15** $35 \div 7$ **16** $36 \div 6$

17 $30 \div 3$ **18** $50 \div 10$ **19** $81 \div 9$ **20** $100 \div 100$

Common Core Mathematics Grade 3 • ©2012 Newmark Learning, LLC

Solve.

1   28 ÷ 4   **2**   72 ÷ 9   **3**   40 ÷ 10   **4**   36 ÷ 9

5   18 ÷ 3   **6**   25 ÷ 5   **7**   24 ÷ 8   **8**   24 ÷ 3

9   30 ÷ 6   **10**   27 ÷ 3   **11**   32 ÷ 8   **12**   48 ÷ 6

13   28 ÷ 4   **14**   49 ÷ 7   **15**   36 ÷ 4   **16**   54 ÷ 6

17   50 ÷ 5   **18**   70 ÷ 10   **19**   64 ÷ 8   **20**   56 ÷ 7

Name _____

Solve.

1 5 x 30

2 20 x 7

3 50 x 9

4 80 x 0

5 70 x 3

6 4 x 60

7 9 x 40

8 80 x 6

9 3 x 90

10 8 x 20

11 30 x 6

12 9 x 10

13 8 x 40

14 50 x 8

15 20 x 9

16 40 x 2

17 0 x 70

18 1 x 50

19 60 x 9

20 80 x 7

Common Core Mathematics Grade 3 • ©2012 Newmark Learning, LLC

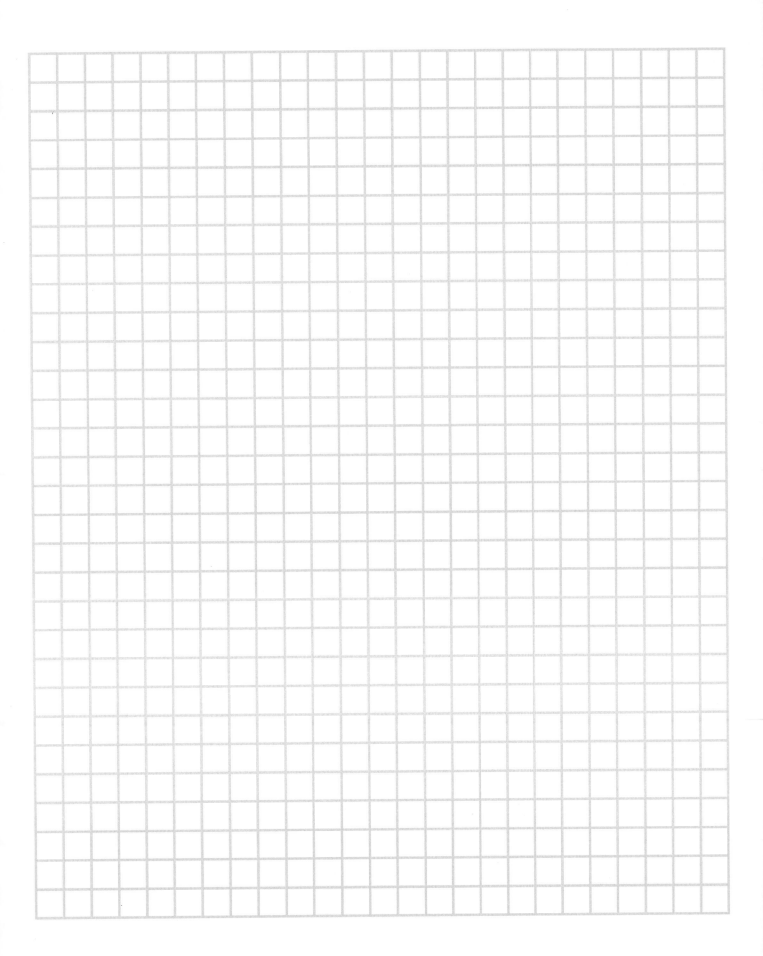

Name _____

x	0	1	2	3	4	5	6	7	8	9	10
0	0	0	0	0	0	0	0	0	0	0	0
1	0	1	2	3	4	5	6	7	8	9	10
2	0	2	4	6	8	10	12	14	16	18	20
3	0	3	6	9	12	15	18	21	24	27	30
4	0	4	8	12	16	20	24	28	32	36	40
5	0	5	10	15	20	25	30	35	40	45	50
6	0	6	12	18	24	30	36	42	48	54	60
7	0	7	14	21	28	35	42	49	56	63	70
8	0	8	16	24	32	40	48	56	64	72	80
9	0	9	18	27	36	45	54	63	72	81	90
10	0	10	20	30	40	50	60	70	80	90	100

Common Core Mathematics Grade 3 • ©2012 Newmark Learning, LLC

Answer Key • Units 1–4

Unit 1 (p. 7) •
1. 60 **2.** 50
3. 110 **4.** 400
5. 300 **6.** 500

Unit 1 (p. 8) ••
1. 620 **2.** 260
3. 400 **4.** 530

5. 800 **6.** 300
7. 600 **8.** 1,000

Unit 1 (p. 9) •••
1. 310; 300
2. 770; 800
3. 450; 500
4. 920; 900

5. 690; 700
6. 70; 100
7. 630; 600
8. 110; 100
9. 550; 600
10. 245–249
11. 940
12. 465–474, 500

Unit 1 (p. 10)
Word Problems
Answers may vary.
1. range: 25–34
2. range: 50–149
3. range: 65–74
4. range: 350–449
5. b **6.** d

Unit 2 (p. 12) •
1. 60 **2.** 50 **3.** 30
4. 100 **5.** 130 **6.** 260
7. 200 **8.** 200 **9.** 200

Unit 2 (p. 13) ••
1. 500 **2.** 90 **3.** 460
4. 50 **5.** 870 **6.** 360
7. 570 **8.** 210 **9.** 960
10. 740 **11.** 540 **12.** 590
13. 250 **14.** 610 **15.** 850

Unit 2 (p. 14) •••
1. 470 **2.** 410 **3.** 620
4. 820 **5.** 170 **6.** 810
7. 720 **8.** 360 **9.** 320
10. 160 **11.** 940 **12.** 710
13. 740 **14.** 660 **15.** 460
16. 690 **17.** 670 **18.** 620
19. 540 **20.** 520

Unit 2 (p. 15)
Word Problems
1. 120 beads
2. 310 baseball cards
3. 290 dollars
4. 220 stickers
5. b
6. c

Unit 3 (p. 17) •
1. 62 **2.** 63
3. 89 **4.** 91
5. 225 **6.** 350

Unit 3 (p. 18) ••
1. 468
2. 269 **3.** 367 **4.** 898
5. 123 **6.** 205 **7.** 304
8. 351 **9.** 801 **10.** 577
11. 569 **12.** 691 **13.** 621
14. 640 **15.** 723 **16.** 972

Unit 3 (p. 19) •••
1. 599 **2.** 250 **3.** 461
4. 886 **5.** 377 **6.** 799
7. 790 **8.** 628 **9.** 975
10. 394 **11.** 716 **12.** 770
13. 762 **14.** 519 **15.** 879
16. 430 **17.** 527 **18.** 581
19. 709 **20.** 821

Unit 3 (p. 20)
Word Problems
1. 507 dollars
2. 971 points
3. 798 craft sticks
4. 602 yards
5. a
6. b

Unit 4 (p. 22) •
1. 21 **2.** 20
3. 39 **4.** 48
5. 23 **6.** 164

Unit 4 (p. 23) ••
1. 215 **2.** 410 **3.** 136
4. 301 **5.** 121 **6.** 319
7. 120 **8.** 45 **9.** 363
10. 371 **11.** 390 **12.** 291
13. 664 **14.** 419

Unit 4 (p. 24) •••
1. 124 **2.** 162 **3.** 375
4. 522 **5.** 189 **6.** 35
7. 336 **8.** 293 **9.** 52
10. 264 **11.** 109 **12.** 373
13. 231 **14.** 82 **15.** 49
16. 117 **17.** 196 **18.** 537
19. 335 **20.** 295

Unit 4 (p. 25)
Word Problems
1. 151 dollars
2. 165 points
3. 77 craft sticks
4. 509 yards
5. b
6. d

Answer Key • Units 5–9

Unit 5 (p. 27) •
1. 3   **2.** 30
3. 27   **4.** 25

Unit 5 (p. 28) ••
1. 9   **2.** 11
3. 7   **4.** 24
5. 16; 8; 24

Unit 5 (p. 29) •••
1. 7   **2.** 5
3. 15   **4.** 11
5. 18; 12; 24
6. 22; 112; 60

Unit 5 (p. 30)
Word Problems
1. 13 pieces of fruit
2. 9 green balloons
3. 5 miles   **4.** 12 muffins
5. a   **6.** d

Unit 6 (p. 32) •
1. 12   **2.** 20
3. 12   **4.** 20
5. 21   **6.** 24

Unit 6 (p. 33) ••
1. 12   **2.** 16
3. 15   **4.** 20
5. 12   **6.** 18

Unit 6 (p. 34) •••
1. 10   **2.** 20
3. 24   **4.** 16
5. 21   **6.** 36

Unit 6 (p. 35)
Word Problems
1. 15 apples
2. 12 plums
3. 18 miles
4. 24 muffins
5. c   **6.** d

Unit 7 (p. 37) •
1. 20   **2.** 30
3. 18   **4.** 32

Unit 7 (p. 38) ••
1. 8   **2.** 24
3. 16   **4.** 20
5. 35   **6.** 54
7. 32   **8.** 21

Unit 7 (p. 39) •••
1. 21   **2.** 32
3. 12   **4.** 24
5. 24   **6.** 18
7. 45   **8.** 18
9. 56   **10.** 72

Unit 7 (p. 40)
Word Problems
1. 56 apples trees
2. 48 corn cobs
3. 20 beets
4. 48 cupcakes
5. d   **6.** b

Unit 8 (p. 42) •
1. 0; 1; 2; 3; 4; 5; 6; 7; 8
2. 0
3. 2; 4; 6; 8; 10; 12; 14;
16
4. 3; 6; 9; 12; 15; 18; 21;
24

Unit 8 (p. 43) ••
1. 8; 10; 12
2. 20; 25; 30
3. 12; 16; 20; 24
4. 4; 12; 24; 30; 36
5. 24; 32; 48
6. 40; 50; 60
7. 6; 9; 12; 15
8. 16; 24; 32; 40

Unit 8 (p. 44) •••
Check students' work.

Unit 8 (p. 45)
Word Problems
1. 0
2. 3
3. multiply by 10
4. c
5. d

Unit 9 (p. 47) •
1. 10, 20, 40, 60, 80
2. 0, 20, 40, 60, 80
3. 30, 60, 90, 40, 80
4. 80, 20, 160, 120, 80
5. 60, 120, 120, 100, 120
6. 160, 140, 160, 60, 160

Unit 9 (p. 48) ••
1. 30, 60, 90, 120, 150
2. 180, 240, 210, 240, 240
3. 120, 180, 90, 180, 240
4. 160, 120, 80, 40, 0
5. 80, 160, 240, 640, 200
6. 240, 320, 200, 280, 320

Unit 9 (p. 49) •••
Check students' work.

Unit 9 (p. 50)
Word Problems
1. 200 dollars
2. 40 points
3. 400; 450; 500
4. d   **5.** b

Common Core Mathematics Grade 3 • ©2012 Newmark Learning, LLC

Answer Key • Units 10–12

Unit 10 (p. 52) •
1. 4   **2.** 5
3. 3   **4.** 4
5. 3   **6.** 7

Unit 10 (p. 53) ••
1. 3   **2.** 4
3. 5; 6; 6   **4.** 32; 4; 8
5. 7; 4; 4   **6.** 48; 6; 8

Unit 10 (p. 54) •••
1. 2, 2   **2.** 3, 4
3. 6, 6   **4.** 5, 5
5. 2, 2   **6.** 7, 7
7. 5, 5   **8.** 4, 4

Unit 10 (p. 55)
Word Problems
1. 6 pizzas
2. 9 trees
3. 3 hours   **4.** 8 horses
5. c   **6.** d

Unit 11 (p. 57) •
1. 3; $3 \times 4 = 12$; $12 \div 3 = 4$
2. 6; $6 \times 5 = 30$; $30 \div 6 = 5$
3. fourth; 5   **4.** first; 8
5. second; 5   **6.** third; 2

Unit 11 (p. 58) ••
1. 20; 4; 5
2. 24; 3; 8
3. $2 \times 7 = 14$; $14 \div 7 = 2$; $14 \div 2 = 7$
4. $6 \times 3 = 18$; $18 \div 6 = 3$; $18 \div 3 = 6$
5. $6 \times 4 = 24$; $24 \div 6 = 4$; $24 \div 4 = 6$
6. $7 \times 5 = 35$; $35 \div 7 = 5$; $35 \div 5 = 7$
7. $9 \times 7 = 63$; $63 \div 7 = 9$; $63 \div 9 = 7$
8. $9 \times 6 = 54$; $54 \div 9 = 6$; $54 \div 6 = 9$

Unit 11 (p. 59) •••
1. 18; 9; 2
2. 24; 8; 3
3. 28; 4; 7
4. 35; 5; 7
5. 36; 4; 9
6. 48; 6; 8
7. $6 \times 5 = 30$; $5 \times 6 = 30$; $30 \div 6 = 5$; $30 \div 5 = 6$
8. $9 \times 3 = 27$; $3 \times 9 = 27$; $27 \div 9 = 3$; $27 \div 3 = 9$
9. $4 \times 6 = 24$; $6 \times 4 = 24$; $24 \div 6 = 4$; $24 \div 4 = 6$
10. $3 \times 7 = 21$; $7 \times 3 = 21$; $21 \div 7 = 3$; $21 \div 3 = 7$
11. $4 \times 8 = 32$; $8 \times 4 = 32$; $32 \div 4 = 8$; $32 \div 8 = 4$
12. $2 \times 8 = 16$; $8 \times 2 = 16$; $16 \div 8 = 2$; $16 \div 2 = 8$

Unit 11 (p. 60)
Word Problems
1. 6 oranges
2. 4 baskets
3. 7 bunches
4. 32 apples
5. c
6. d

Unit 12 (p. 62) •
1. 18   **2.** 40
3. 12   **4.** 32

Unit 12 (p. 63) ••
1. 5   **2.** 25
3. 8   **4.** 16
5. 4   **6.** 3

Unit 12 (p. 64) •••
1. 15   **2.** 48
3. 3   **4.** 42
5. 6   **6.** 24
7. 5   **8.** 4

Unit 12 (p. 65)
Word Problems
1. 16 shoes
2. 4 pans
3. 54 blocks
4. 7 apples
5. d
6. b

Answer Key • Units 13–16

Unit 13 (p. 67) •
1. 6   **2.** 12
3. 24   **4.** 7
5. 4   **6.** 6

Unit 13 (p. 68) ••
1. 3   **2.** 30
3. 8   **4.** 4
5. 7   **6.** 6
7. 9   **8.** 6

Unit 13 (p. 69) •••
1. 2   **2.** 3
3. 5   **4.** 4
5. 30   **6.** 4
7. 4   **8.** 9
9. 4   **10.** 7
11. 6   **12.** 9

Unit 13 (p. 70)
Word Problems
1. 9 pairs of socks
2. 9 turnip plants
3. 4 apples
4. 9 sandwiches
5. d
6. c

Unit 14 (p. 72) •
1. 2   **2.** 3; 1
3. 4; 4   **4.** 8; 8
5. 8; 8   **6.** 3; 3

Unit 14 (p. 73) ••
1. 1/4   **2.** 1/3
3. 2/3   **4.** 1/2
5. 2/8   **6.** 1/8
7. 2/4   **8.** 1/2

Unit 14 (p. 74) •••
1. 3   **2.** 3
3. 5; 4/5   **4.** 2; 2/2
5. 1   **6.** 2
7. 5; 2/5   **8.** 2; 1/2

Unit 14 (p. 75)
Word Problems
1. 1/2
2. 1/3
3. 3/4
4. 3/8
5. d
6. d

Unit 15 (p. 77) •
1. halves
2. fourths
3. thirds
4. eighths
5. sixths

Unit 15 (p. 78) ••
Check students' work.

Unit 15 (p. 79) •••
1. 1/4   **2.** 4/4
3. 1/3   **4.** 2/3
5. 4/6   **6.** 1/6
7. 3/8   **8.** 7/8
9. 2/6   **10.** 3/6
11. 5/8   **12.** 1/8

Unit 15 (p. 80)
Word Problems
1. 1/4; 3/4
2. 1/2
3. 1/3; 2/3; 3/3
4. a

Unit 16 (p. 82) •
1. 2   **2.** 2
3. 2   **4.** 4
5. 4   **6.** 6

Unit 16 (p. 83) ••
Answers may vary.
1. 2/6   **2.** 4/6
3. 6/6   **4.** 2/4
5. 2/8   **6.** 6/8
7. 1/4   **8.** 1/2
9. 3/4   **10.** 1/5
11. 2/5   **12.** 3/5

Unit 16 (p. 84) •••
Answers may vary.
1. 4/6   **2.** 2/8
3. 4/10   **4.** 1/2
5. 2/2   **6.** 3/4
7. 4/10   **8.** 2/4
9. 3/3   **10.** 3/5
11. 2/3   **12.** 1/2
13. 1/4   **14.** 2/6
15. 8/10

Unit 16 (p. 85)
Word Problems
1. 4
2. 3
3. 10
4. 8
5. d
6. d

Common Core Mathematics Grade 3 • ©2012 Newmark Learning, LLC

Answer Key • Units 17–20

Unit 17 (p. 87) •
1. < 2. >
3. < 4. <
5. < 6. >
7. < 8. =

Unit 17 (p. 88) ••
1. > 2. <
3. < 4. >
5. > 6. <
7. < 8. >
9. < 10. <
11. > 12. >

Unit 17 (p. 89) •••
Answers may vary.
1. 2 2. 3
3. 2 4. 3
5. 1 6. 2
7. 4 8. 4
9. 1/3 10. 2/8
11. 2/5 12. >
13. 1/4 14. 1/2
15. 3/4

Unit 17 (p. 90)
Word Problems
1. <; 5/8; pepperoni
2. Jamie
3. Wednesday
4. Jake
5. a
6. c

Unit 18 (p. 92) •
1. 3:20; 3
2. 10:24; 24
3. 8:39; 39
4. 6:30; 6
5. 10:30; 10
6. 11:18; 18

Unit 18 (p. 93) ••
1. 7:03; 3
2. 9:28; 28; 9
3. 11:47; 12
4. 1:56; 4; 2; 2:06
5. 4:11; 11; 4; 4:21
6. 5:48; 12; 6; 5:58

Unit 18 (p. 94) •••
1. 2:05; 2:15
2. 9:42; 9:52
3. 1:11; 1:21
4. 3:52; 4:02
5. 6:35; 6:45
6. 10:02; 10:12
7. 4:57; 5:07
8. 8:23; 8:33

Unit 18 (p. 95)
Word Problems
1. 22 2. 15
3. 16 4. 9
5. 32 6. 12
7. 18 8. 53

Unit 19 (p. 97) •
1. Check students' work.
2. Check student's work.

Unit 19 (p. 98) ••
1. 1 kilogram
2. 1 gram
3. 10 kilograms
4. 200 kilograms
5. 1 liter
6. 5 liters
7. 50 liters
8. 3 liters

Unit 19 (p. 99) •••
Check students' work.

Unit 19 (p. 100)
Word Problems
1. less than a liter
2. less than a liter
3. 3 liters
4. 20 liters
5. d
6. b

Unit 20 (p. 102) •
1. 3 1/4
2. 4 3/4
3. 2
4. 5
5. 2 2/4
6. 4 1/4

Unit 20 (p. 103) ••
1. 4 2. 3 1/4
3. 3 3/4 4. 3 3/4
5. 3 1/2 6. 3
7. 3 1/2 8. 3 3/4
9. Check students' work.

Unit 20 (p. 104) •••
Check students' work.

Unit 20 (p. 105)
Word Problems
1. Check students' work.
2. c
3. d

Answer Key • Units 21–24

Unit 21 (p. 107) •
1. apple
2. 2
3. 5
4. 6

Unit 21 (p. 108) ••
1. Check students' work.
2. 2
3. 4
4. 6
5. Check students' work.
6. 2
7. 7
8. 5

Unit 21 (p. 109)
•••
1. Check students' work.
2. 7
3. 2
4. 8
5. Check students' work.
6. 3
7. 6
8. 0

Unit 21 (p. 110)
Word Problems
1. Check students' work.
2. 5
3. 10
4. 5
5. Check students' work.
6. 1
7. 3
8. 2

Unit 22 (p. 112) •
1. 1
2. 5
3. 7
4. 3

Unit 22 (p. 113) ••
1. 3
2. 4
3. 1
4. 8

Unit 22 (p. 114)•••
1. Check students' work.
2. 2
3. 5
4. 7
5. Check students' work.
6. 5
7. 35
8. 155

Unit 22 (p. 115)
Word Problems
1. Check students' work.
2. bologna and ham
3. 3
4. 2
5. Check students' work.
6. 50   7. 200
8. 350

Unit 23 (p. 117) •
1. 12
2. 10
3. 8
4. 12

Unit 23 (p. 118) ••
Check students' work.

Unit 23 (p. 119)•••
1. 16   2. 9
3. 14   4. 18
5. 12   6. 20

Unit 23 (p. 120)
Word Problems
1. 22 units
2. 64 units
3. 70 feet
4. 50 meters
5. b   6. b

Unit 24 (p. 122) •
1. 8   2. 7
3. 16   4. 10
5. 6   6. 16

Unit 24 (p. 123) ••
Check students' work.

Unit 24 (p. 124)•••
1. 12; 12
2. 5; 2; 10; 10
3. 15   4. 28
5. 30   6. 16

Unit 24 (p. 125)
Word Problems
1. 24 square units
2. 25 square units
3. 80 square feet
4. 10 square meters
5. d   6. c

Common Core Mathematics Grade 3 • ©2012 Newmark Learning, LLC

Answer Key • Unit 25–27

Unit 25 (p. 127) •

1. 10   2. 7
3. 16   4. 6
5. 15   6. 16

Unit 25 (p. 128) ••

1. 12   2. 5, 2; 10
3. 3 x 5 =; 15
4. 7 x 4 =; 28
5. 6 x 5 =; 30
6. 4 x 4 =; 16

Unit 25 (p. 129)•••

1. 8   2. 12
3. 15 square units
4. 24 square units
5. 24 square units
6. 40 - 18 = 22 square units

Unit 25 (p. 130)

Word Problems
1. 24 square meters
2. 150 square feet
3. 180 square inches
4. 600 square centimeters
5. b
6. c

Unit 26 (p. 132) •

Check students' work.

Unit 26 (p. 133) ••

Check students' work.

Unit 26 (p. 134)•••

Check students' work.

Unit 26 (p. 135)

Word Problems
Check students' work.

Unit 27 (p. 137) •

Check students' work.

Unit 27 (p. 138) ••

Check students' work.

Unit 27 (p. 139)•••

Check students' work.

Unit 27 (p. 140)

Word Problems
Check students' work.
1. 30 square units
2. 9 square units
3. 20 square units
4. 16 square units
5. 24 square units
6. 48 square units

Answer Key • Fluency Practice

p. 141

1. 560; 600	**5.** 710; 700	**9.** 930; 900	**12.** 545–554; Answers may vary.
2. 340; 300	**6.** 350; 300	**10.** 445–449	
3. 280; 300	**7.** 460; 500	**11.** 640; 600	
4. 120; 100	**8.** 830; 800		

p. 142

1. 325	**6.** 293	**11.** 690	**16.** 372
2. 567	**7.** 603	**12.** 358	**17.** 527
3. 384	**8.** 664	**13.** 804	**18.** 820
4. 881	**9.** 850	**14.** 290	**19.** 235
5. 13	**10.** 240	**15.** 802	**20.** 406

p. 143

1. 214	**6.** 163	**11.** 838	**16.** 472
2. 120	**7.** 278	**12.** 895	**17.** 400
3. 541	**8.** 555	**13.** 430	**18.** 437
4. 840	**9.** 741	**14.** 49	**19.** 65
5. 9	**10.** 38	**15.** 51	**20.** 305

p. 144

1. 35	**6.** 63	**11.** 10	**16.** 30
2. 9	**7.** 20	**12.** 8	**17.** 18
3. 12	**8.** 24	**13.** 8	**18.** 40
4. 32	**9.** 60	**14.** 54	**19.** 10
5. 12	**10.** 0	**15.** 28	**20.** 63

p. 145

1. 15	**6.** 24	**11.** 18	**16.** 8
2. 14	**7.** 36	**12.** 9	**17.** 0
3. 45	**8.** 48	**13.** 80	**18.** 5
4. 0	**9.** 27	**14.** 40	**19.** 20
5. 21	**10.** 16	**15.** 18	**20.** 56

p. 146

1. 80	**6.** 0	**11.** 54	**16.** 21
2. 42	**7.** 40	**12.** 18	**17.** 36
3. 9	**8.** 16	**13.** 63	**18.** 4
4. 90	**9.** 48	**14.** 60	**19.** 100
5. 49	**10.** 25	**15.** 81	**20.** 64

p. 147

1. 3	**6.** 7	**11.** 4	**16.** 9
2. 1	**7.** 5	**12.** 8	**17.** 6
3. 1	**8.** 6	**13.** 5	**18.** 4
4. 2	**9.** 3	**14.** 7	**19.** 1
5. 3	**10.** 0	**15.** 6	**20.** 3

p. 148

1. 2	**6.** 2	**11.** 7	**16.** 6
2. 2	**7.** 7	**12.** 4	**17.** 10
3. 10	**8.** 6	**13.** 2	**18.** 5
4. 5	**9.** 4	**14.** 9	**19.** 9
5. 8	**10.** 3	**15.** 5	**20.** 1

p. 149

1. 7	**6.** 5	**11.** 4	**16.** 9
2. 8	**7.** 3	**12.** 8	**17.** 10
3. 4	**8.** 8	**13.** 7	**18.** 7
4. 4	**9.** 5	**14.** 7	**19.** 8
5. 6	**10.** 9	**15.** 9	**20.** 8

p. 150

1. 150	**6.** 240	**11.** 180	**16.** 80
2. 140	**7.** 360	**12.** 90	**17.** 0
3. 450	**8.** 480	**13.** 320	**18.** 50
4. 0	**9.** 270	**14.** 400	**19.** 540
5. 210	**10.** 160	**15.** 180	**20.** 560

Common Core Mathematics Grade 3 • ©2012 Newmark Learning, LLC